Jen Sincero

a fireside book
published by simon & schuster
new york   london   toronto   sydney

the
straight
girl's
guide
to
sleeping

with

chicks

*Names and other characteristics of some
individuals in this book have been changed.*

FIRESIDE
Rockefeller Center
1230 Avenue of the Americas
New York, NY 10020

For information regarding special discounts for bulk purchases,
please contact Simon & Schuster Special Sales at 1-800-456-6798
or business@simonandschuster.com

Designed by Jaime Putorti

Manufactured in the United States of America

10 9 8 7 6 5 4 3

Library of Congress Cataloging-in-Publication Data
Control Number: 2004058468

ISBN 0-7432-5853-3

To the Big Guy
and
Mr. Squirrely Jones

contents

introduction

The Joy of Sex with Chicks

I think my first sexual encounter with a member of the same sex happened when I was seven. My friend Wendy and I would spend hours playing with these little plastic Fisher-Price people who came with cars and houses and villages and stuff. We'd make up stories about them, have them go to work and cook dinner, and when they were bad we'd send them off to The Big Ween. "Uh-oh, Sally didn't do her homework again," Wendy would say, kicking off her panties and lying on the floor. She'd hold terrified little plastic Sally up in the air and announce to the entire Fisher-Price community that "Sally was bad and must go to The Big Ween," then slowly lower the toy between her legs. I'd watch mesmerized as Wendy rubbed Sally around and around, stopping only when Wendy's My First Pussy had gotten its fill. Inevitably, moments later, my own Mr. Smith would wind up telling a lie or robbing the Fisher-Price bank and my panties would go flying across the room. "Uhhhh-ohhhhhh!"

I'm not sure if this counts as sex, since there were actually two The Big Weens, Wendy overseeing operations at hers and me at mine, but I do know that for me it wasn't all innocent play. I was a really sexual kid who started masturbating at around five years old, and who was constantly getting sent to my room for greeting company with my hand down my pants. So I find it kind of surprising, since I was such an early enthusiast and a curious person in general, that it took me until my thirties to really get down and dirty with another woman. I'd done my fair share of dabbling, made out with a few drunk friends, and groped the occasional boob here and there, but nothing all that intimate ever happened. It was usually the result of being wasted and figuring that if there were no cute guys around I might as well pin Sharon to the couch. And it never went beyond that until my thirties. Maybe I was too uptight or too immature, or maybe all my friends were just uglier back then—whatever the reason, it took me a couple decades before I found myself face to face with The Big

Ween again. And much to my surprise, just like little plastic Sally, I got sucked in by it.

At the risk of never getting laid again, I decided I'd write a book, because my experiences with women affected me in such a radical and positive way I had to make sure other women knew about it. I wanted everyone who's ever thought about it to try it. So what if I repelled future lovers, terrified that their most intimate secrets might wind up somewhere on page 84?

It was like I'd learned a whole new language that suddenly allowed me to communicate with members of my own gender in a way I never had before. As if sex wasn't already fabulous enough, I'd just doubled my fun by transforming the other half of the population into possible bedmates. It did incredible things for my confidence as a woman and as a sexual being, and whether or not I ever meet a woman I want to sleep with again, I'm really grateful I've done it. Several things in particular about the experience really struck me, because they were so remarkably different from being with a guy:

1. When you're with another chick, the roles can switch back and forth in a much more equal and fluid way than they do with a guy. You can be the butch one, totally in control, throwing her around in

bed, and then switch to being submissive and girly. It obviously depends on who you're sleeping with, since many women identify with being more dominant or submissive and aren't up for flippy-flopping, but if you get with someone who hasn't chosen sides you can switch back and forth and feel fully in either role, which I find incredibly hot. This is not to say that you can't do something similar with men—I've been with some stunningly open and experimental guys—but even if you put them in a dress, strap them down, and make them call you Daddy, they still have a dick and you still have a pussy, which automatically makes them more masculine and you more feminine. Without that biological reality, you're totally free to be whatever, and I found it incredibly liberating and exciting to really feel one hundred percent on both sides.

2. The way women orgasm is so different from the way guys do. We don't need to stop and recharge before starting up again, so we can go on and on till the break of dawn without a time-out. I've never in my life had nonstop sessions like the ones I had with girls. It's crazy! It can bring you to a state of prolonged excitement that's almost unbearable. There were times when I seriously thought I was going to have a heart attack.

3. I found that every time I did something to *her*, I could imagine I was doing it to myself. So much so that I could practically feel it even if I wasn't touching myself at all. The combo of watching her get off and imagining exactly what it must feel like could bring me to orgasm.

4. Women's bodies are unbelievably soft! They're like the softest pillows in the world. This has made me totally understand why men go apeshit over us. It also made me aware of my own body's softness, and it made me feel incredibly sexy in a way I never had before.

5. Lastly, because we live in a society that has a large stick up its ass, and also because my sexual hometown is Straightyville, sleeping with someone I wasn't "supposed" to made me feel kind of kinky. This turned me on like nobody's business. I felt a teeny bit nasty, dirty, and queer, and I think this helped inspire me to step outside my sexual box more than I ever had before. I did stuff with girls that I'd always wanted to try—we went to sex clubs, tied each other up, dabbled in S&M, and enjoyed the wide world of sex toys. I attribute a large part of this to the fact that I was with like-minded kinky and adventurous souls whom I trusted and who I was

sexually compatible with. But also, the fact that they were women broke the dam of my usual sexual behavior and opened me up to a flood of new experiences.

The whole thing was so inspiring I immediately started handing out surveys and interviewing other people to hear their stories and to get all angles. The more women I talked to, the more I learned that sleeping with chicks was either on the majority's to do list or already crossed off. Even the people who really looked like respectable, take-yourself-and-your-filthy-questionnaire-off-my-property types were game. And I have to say that the majority of them gave the whole experience an enthusiastic two thumbs up. They couldn't wait to spill the beans to me—in graphic detail, I might add—and I couldn't get over how inspiring it was to learn that all these women are out there fearlessly pushing the sexual envelope. Girls are curious. Girls are hot. Chicks dig 'em!

When looking for people to survey, I cast as wide a net as possible. Tons of different factors go into determining how we approach sex in general: religion, age, parental influence, general uptightness, tequila shots . . . In the fifties you saved yourself for marriage, while today everyone's starting to screw at an age once associated with hopscotch and noogies. Asking the same questions of people from different planets resulted in a wide variety of answers. And I'd like to say I represented all groups equally, but I'm afraid I didn't—most of the women in the over-seventy-years-old demographic whom I dared approach treated me like a filthy whore, so I wasn't able to get as wide an age range as I would have liked.

I spoke with straight chicks who've slept with straight chicks; straight chicks who've slept with lesbians; straight chicks who've done both or neither or were too drunk to remember; lesbians who've slept with straight chicks; bisexuals; undecideds; and my mother. I put up flyers on college campuses, online, in bars, and in the lobby of a nursing home. One underlying theme kept repeating itself: women connect with women. We can talk to women easily, relate to their issues, process our "stuff" and provide emotional support on a level that suggests a deep spiritual connection. I know this is a big fat generalization—certainly there are women I'd rather kick into an empty pool than talk to for three minutes—but in general there's an emotional language specific to women that creates a certain bond. And when you take the leap and bring good old sex into this equation, it can really make your hair stand up. Whether you're slamming Mary in the bathroom stall or picking out china patterns with Tiffany, you stand to touch on something deeper than you may have counted on.

This fact kind of tossed a monkey wrench into my plan. I'd set out to write a funny, sexy, sassy book that people could give as a gift or leave on their coffee tables to liven up a cocktail party. Something that people could flip through, laugh at, and slap their hand over their mouths, squealing, "Oh my god, my husband and I tag-teamed our nanny, *too!*" I do believe I accomplished this, but really delving into the subject of sex with chicks made me realize that there's a whole lot more I needed to talk about. Sex is heavy, and sex with women can be as deep as it is liberating. It allows us to break free of heterosexual roles and expectations and explore sex in a whole new way. We get to experience a similar body that'll give us incredible insights into our own. The fact that I'd overcome my inhibitions about being with women opened me up to trying things with them that I was too shy to try with a guy. It made anything possible, and I know I'm a better lover today because of it.

Another thing that may take some by surprise is that it's possible to become attached even if you're "straight." If your experience lasts longer than a happy hour, it can have the added extra weight of the aforementioned female bonding. If you're having hot sex with a chick on a regular basis, chances are very good you're also connecting with her emotionally, which can totally screw up the free-and-easy "I'm not hungry, I'll just pick" position we straight girls can go at it from. In fact, it's not at all uncommon for straight women to get into committed, monogamous relationships with other women. "It was total addiction from the get-go," says Carrie, 41. "We were madly in love. I felt a certain connection and understanding with her that I never got with any man. When we broke up, it was more for personality reasons than the fact that she was a woman."

As for my own experience with dating women, I was more confused than committed. I'd never had crushes on women, never done my signature calling-and-hanging-up routine, never turned down a piece of chocolate cake because thoughts of Amanda had filled my stomach with butterflies. Then, all of a sudden, I found myself with an incredible woman who got it and me, and the sex was hot as hell, and before I knew it I was in a relationship. I'd never connected with anyone the way I did with her, and that definitely articulated itself sexually as well. She listened to me as no guy ever did and she totally knew where I was coming from. If I was weeping at a commercial, instead of looking at me as if I was insane she'd grab me a tissue. She understood my mood swings and my feelings, and could fully articulate her own. I felt nurtured and safe and understood. But—unfortunately—I wouldn't/couldn't/didn't get all the way in. Because although there's no questioning that I loved her, the feeling lacked a certain tug I was used to feeling for guys. Granted, I've felt that tug for guys who live in their cars and refuse to hold my hand in public, but I need the tug. It marks the difference between someone you're crazy about and someone you're in love with. At least, that's what I kept telling myself. Was I using the tug as an excuse because I was scared to be with a woman for real? Was I tugless because she just wasn't the one? Am I just a big fat dick-lovin' whore and that's that?

It didn't help that I was constantly being bombarded with questions along the lines of "So, like, are you a lesbian now, or what?" It's the first thing that everybody asked me when I told them I was seeing a chick, and it brings up a question that needs to be addressed. What the hell does it mean to be straight or gay or bi or whatever? And why does it matter?

Labels are indeed for cans and for lazy authors, and for people who are generally uncomfy without everything being put in neat little boxes. Labels are hopelessly point-less. I know several women who were out and proud and fully lesbian identified for decades who are now allegedly Mrs. John Straightypants. Then there are women who were once staunch straights who are now shacking up with chicks. There are bisexual women who like fucking gay boys, gay men who like fucking women who used to be men, people who dress up like stuffed animals and fuck each other, and on and on and on. It's murky out there in sexland. Humans have been screwing anything that'll hold still long enough since the beginning of time, and trying to figure out what and why in order to catalogue it all is a big fat waste of time.

But I have a book to write here and I need to identify people somehow.

Ideally this book would be titled *A Guide for Women Who Usually Have Sexual Relationships with Men and Who Would Now Like to Explore Sexual Relationships and/or Brief Encounters with Women.* Instead I'm going to be a hypocrite and fall back on using the standard labels I so enjoy looking down upon. I hope that everyone who reads this assumes the definition in my ideal title is what I'm talking about when I say "straight" (I also refuse to put quotes around the word "straight" for the duration of the book). This may sound nitpicky, but the world of sexual identification is a vast and political one that most heteros are completely oblivious to, since we haven't had to go to battle with popular opinion over our sexual preferences. Those of you who decide to step over the heterosexual boundaries may get an unexpected taste of how the other half lives. You may suddenly be challenged by the heterosexual, bisexual, and homosexual communities to define your sexuality, and chastised when you don't adhere to certain rules. You may also find that you're suddenly demanding some explanations from yourself.

For the majority of women I spoke with, however, leaving the warm, secure confines of Hetero World was totally worth it. "You get to have this thrill ride with something taboo," one experienced dabbler explained. "It's like a secret weapon that ups your sexual confidence. It made me feel really powerful. And tingly. There's something really sublime about connecting with another woman that way." "There's something about a woman's body that's just so sensual," another wannabe said. "It seems kind of safe and terrifying at the same time." I spoke with women who fantasize about sex with women but have no interest in making it happen, those who only want to do it to please their boyfriends, and one experienced lady who said: "I'll fuck anything when I'm drunk."

Whatever your reasons may be, you certainly have nothing to lose by trying it. For me, sleeping with a woman was like taking a superhero pill. It inspired interesting discussions with friends, family, and a slew of strangers. It opened me up to the incredibly diverse world of sexuality that I'd only dipped my toe into before and which I'm now fascinated by. As with anything else in life that intrigues you, you'll feel a lot worse for never trying it than you will for trying it and having it not work out. Why die wondering?

chapter one

Curiosity Didn't Kill the Pussy; It Only Made Her Stronger

My first time being with a woman I was super excited—you hear about this stuff all the time, you're curious, and when you finally get to see what's it's really like it's awesome! I was so glad I finally found out.

—SUSAN, 20

One of the excellent things about being a straight chick is that we can fool around with members of our own sex without it being some big huge deal. If you find yourself sitting at a bar one night, surrounded by empty shot glasses, molesting someone named Janice, you have nothing to worry about. Chances are you'll wake up the next day and giggle about it with your friends while you sift through a towering pile of cocktail napkins containing the numbers of every guy in the bar. This is because, even in our good ol' homophobic society, the idea of two chicks getting it on is met with a resounding "Fuck yeah!" by the majority of the straight male population. In fact, this is one of the precious few instances where a double standard actually works in our favor. A man's masculinity is threatened by same-sex experimentation while a woman's femininity is supersized; the line "I fucked a dude!" coming out of a football player's mouth falls like a brick, while "I fucked a chick!" floats like a soap bubble from the lips of a cheerleader. This is obviously as heinous as any other double standard, and the world would benefit greatly from dudes playing a little footsie with each other every once in a while, but it's a double standard that benefits all us curious spinsters, bitches, and sluts by creating a carefree environment to experiment in.

"It was one of the most liberating things I've ever done," says Elizabeth, 42, happily married. "I was twenty-five, sitting on the couch watching TV with my friend. She was pretty butch and I knew all about her life and stuff, but I never really gave it much thought as something I'd want to try myself. Then all of a sudden, bam, she just leaped on me! At first I was like, 'What the hell are you doing?,' but it was so unexpected and exciting . . . it sent this huge rush through my whole body. We ended up being together for a year. It was really good for me. I think being with a woman can be a very nurturing experience." Others say it was "totally mind-blowing!," "surprisingly hot," and "very liberating." In a survey I took of straight women who've tried it, 90 percent gave it a thumbs-up, 8 percent a thumbs down, 2 percent were undecided, and one sourpuss said: "I lost one of my best friends. I'm never hitting that shit again." And if you do it for no other reason, do it because it's hip.

famous straight women who've dabbled

Madonna	Sinéad O'Connor
Britney Spears	Frida Kahlo
Anne Heche	Ally McBeal
Eleanor Roosevelt	Kim Cattrall
Xena	Drew Barrymore
Ally Sheedy	Angelina Jolie
Ione Skye	Lisa Marie Presley
Janice Dickerson	Margaret Cho
	Cynthia Nixon

Even with such a high rate of customer satisfaction, exploring the unknown scares the poop out of some people. Fear. Is there anything more tired? As my great-grandmother always said: "You're a much bigger douchebag for not trying something than for trying it and fucking it up." The satisfaction of knowing you had the cojones to face your fears far outweighs whatever the minuses may be. And when it comes to sleeping with chicks, you get that satisfaction *plus* an orgasm, *plus* you kind of feel like a stud. Here are some of the more common obstacles that hold curious women back.

"I'm Hot For Her, I'm Hot For Her Not"

If you've never done it before, how can you really be sure you want to get it on with a chick? "What if I light a bunch of vanilla candles, play Barry White ever so softly in the background, slowly lower her into my rose-petaled bathtub, and wind up bone dry? How can I avoid setting myself up for that kind of humiliation?" When it comes to pursuing your bisexuality, don't let uncertainty become a chastity belt. It's like any decision you have to make where your true feelings are a tad fuzzy. Do I want cheekless leather chaps or is it just because they're on sale? Am I hungry or just bored? Are chicks hot or did my boyfriend just forget my birthday again? In any case, knowledge and objectivity are the best tools. To clear up any confusion before taking the big plunge, you should first check to see if you're a likely candidate.

☞ *10 Tell-tale Signs That You Aspire to Sex with Another Woman:*

1. When you get drunk, you think about making out with chicks.
2. When you get drunk you make out with chicks.
3. You've pretended he's a woman when he's doing that to you down there.
4. You've masturbated to the thought of three gorgeous women servicing you in a bathtub.
5. You've caught yourself casually flipping through the "Women Seeking Women" section of the personals more than once.

6. When your boyfriend brings up having a three-way with another woman, you're more excited about it than he is.
7. You'll go see any movie with Angelina Jolie in it.
8. When you hang out with your lesbian friends, you feel like you're missing out.
9. Titty bars are hot; Chippendales is not.
10. Your eyes have lingered a little too long while you were helping your best friend try on bras.

sleeping with chicks old wives' tale #1:

**If you're fed up with men,
you'll automatically be attracted to women.**

The Virgin Jitters

Then there's the whole losing your virginity thing and all the what-if-I-suck-in-bed trauma that goes along with that. Four words: Mas. Tur. Ba. Tion. Practice makes perfect, and you were born with the perfect practice space. It's not like your first time with a guy when you fumbled around, dropping balls right and left, while you desperately tried to read the mind of the one-eyed pokeman (Is it happy? Is it sad? Oh, God, why is it shrinking?). With a woman you can do some research ahead of time, study the control panels until you know them like the back of your hand. I recommend sitting down and really thinking about what turns you on, where you like to be touched, how you like it touched by lips, fingers, tongue, whatever, and then imagine how you'd go about doing that to another woman. Picture the room, what you're wearing, what you're feeling, what you want to do to her, and then practice your moves on yourself. Chapter 2, "The Super-Huge Importance of Sticking Your Hand Down Your Pants," delves more deeply into the countless benefits of masturbation, but it deserves mention here as a great way to ease your mind. In general, think of good sex as if you're giving someone the perfect gift. Your best bet is to give them something you really want for yourself.

Another thing that might help is talking to your straight-guy or lesbian friends. One good word of advice can go a long way; if your friends have had any success in the sack, chances are they can help you out. I also recommend reading up on the subject—check out some of the books I list in the back of this one. There's plenty of good lesbian erotica to choose from. And remember, this is just sex with another person. It's not some huge big deal, so don't psych yourself out. Have fun with it. Treat the mystery of sleeping with another woman the way you would the mystery of sleeping with anyone new for the first time. Male or female, there are always question marks and exciting discoveries.

The Paparazzi

The terror of someone finding out is another reason more girl-on-girl sex isn't happening. If this is a major concern for you, you should only sleep with people you know and trust, who do not have big mouths. And you should only do it in places where neither of your cars will be recognized. If you're going for straight girls, you should leave it up to them to make the first move, because if you hit on them and they freak out, it'll be easier to count the people who don't know about it than those who do. Going for lesbians in this case is a much safer bet since your chances of scoring are much higher, as lesbians tend to make a habit of sleeping with other chicks. But again, make sure it isn't with someone who has a bullhorn for a mouth. And whatever you do, don't get drunk in public with chicks you're attracted to. Not only will people find out that you're messing around with women, but many of them will have firsthand accounts or, even worse, pictures.

sleeping with chicks tip #1

Alcohol is a gateway drug to sleeping
with members of the same sex.

Paranormal Paranoia

Some people can't let go for fear that a dead mother or father is watching. Others worry that God will shake his almighty finger at them. These people probably don't masturbate either, nor do they steal stuff from work, venture outside the missionary position, or break something and then carefully put it back so that the next person who comes along will think *they* broke it. Worrying about the supernatural is a full-time job, and I have no idea how these people survive. All I can say is that if it were me, I'd figure that if my dead parents and God have a problem with me, they have only themselves to blame. After all, they created me, and this is who I am. If they get to be all high and mighty about lugging me around for nine months and only taking one day off a week just so I could exist, they get all the responsibilities that come with those honors, too. Then I'd do some research and find out exactly how many people have been stricken down dead by God for sleeping with a member of the same sex. If it's a number I could deal with, I'd just go ahead and take my chances. I would also go to therapy.

Waking Up Your Inner Lesbo

Another big fear for some is that an innocent visit to the other side of town will turn into a desire to relocate completely. And then what the hell are you supposed to do? "It's not like you've changed your hair color and all of a sudden you have to go out and buy all these new lipstick shades," one woman dubiously pointed out. "You'd have to change everything, and I'm just not willing to go through that kind of overhaul." Being gay in this society can be a big pain in the ass, but being too lame to do the things that make you happy is worse. Unfortunately, being lame is a way of life for some people. They feel at the top of their game when all aspects of their true selves are safely tucked away, slowly suffocating behind a wall of fake contentment. If this sounds familiar, then sex with another woman probably isn't for you: anyone who's that uptight about liking it too much most likely will. You need to first deal with a much larger issue: that you are a weenie. If you don't tackle this first, there's no way you'll be able to partake in any sort of girl-on-girl escapade and have it be a positive experience.

If you recognize yourself in any of these descriptions do not despair. You've just completed the first step in overcoming your fears, which is identifying them. Once you know what they are, you can go about bulldozing past them. Remember, fear is all bark and no bite. All you have to do is face fear head on and it'll run away whimpering with its tail between its legs. Think about something that used to terrify you, something that you got used to and that now you don't think twice about before doing. Things are rarely as scary as you build them up to be, and once you deal with them, it's easy to see how the fear was all in your mind. If you don't let fear get in your way, you'll be a big fat girl-slut before you know it.

> I think my being with a woman was very eye-opening for a lot of my friends. They heard about the great sex I was having and how well we connected and were like, "I'm going out and getting myself a chick too!"
>
> —CARRIE, 41

chapter two

The Super-Huge Importance of Sticking Your Hand Down Your Pants

It really bugs me that I allowed someone else access to my body sexually before I knew how to make myself come. Now that I know what I like, I feel much more empowered.

—DANA, 25

arely is anyone all that great at anything without a little practice first. And when it comes to fuckin', anyone with a little spare alone time and arms long enough to reach her crotch has all she needs to get an education. Granted, masturbating is a far cry from the real deal, but if you really hunker down and do the work you'll absolutely get results. No matter who you're sleeping with. And when it comes to girl-on-girl sex, the better you know yourself, the better you'll be able to please her.

This is such an important topic that I can't write about

it without first addressing an alarming discovery I made while gathering information for this book: there's a butt-load of women out there who are too freaked out to masturbate. Who feel too ashamed or pathetic or, who, as one woman put it, "wouldn't even know where to begin." What's up with that? These are real live grown-up fabulous confident women! Most of these women say they've never had an orgasm, either. And the fact that they're not masturbating has a whole lot to do with it.

Unlike the male orgasm, which is fairly automatic, the female orgasm takes more coaxing and concentration—when's the last time you heard a guy complain, "She came way before I did, fell asleep, and I ended up finishing myself off"? A female orgasm can be aloof, temperamental, and mysterious, and she can take a while to show up, if she decides to show up at all. Most of us need to learn how to orgasm by figuring out which combination of fantasy, touch, and concentration works for us. This can absolutely be done with a lover, but if it's not happening, women need to do their homework—and feel okay about doing it! The fact that anyone is missing out on an orgasmic life because she's too ashamed to touch herself makes me so sad. And pissed off. In a world where men jerk off in public, how can it be that there's still such a wall of silence and shame surrounding the practice of female masturbation?

I'd say it has something to do with the fact that women have forever been made to feel that our sexual pleasure is less significant and acceptable than men's is. When it comes to masturbation, the old slut-versus-stud double standard strikes again. Men get to be very matter-of-fact about masturbating; most of them talk about it as if they're talking about washing their cars. It's so not a big deal that it's even managed to become a part of our everyday vocabulary, both as a noun ("Look what that jerk-off did to my truck!") and as a verb ("We blew off work and pretty much just jerked off at the beach all day"). And there's clearly a certain quota of nut-grabbing every rap video must meet before it's allowed to air. Meanwhile female masturbation was locked away in a dank forgotten basement the moment she was born, like an embarrassing family secret. This is not to say that society doesn't provide plenty of shame and repression regarding masturbation and sex in general regardless of your gender, because it does. But the ladies definitely bear the brunt, and it affects everything from how we orgasm to how we see ourselves in the world.

That anyone should be scolded for the harmless pursuit of simple pleasures is just plain mean. And it seems like we girls get in trouble for having fun all the time—don't eat that, don't wear that, don't get paid that, don't say that, don't be good at that, don't fuck that unless I can watch . . . it's like everything we do is up on trial, even what we do in the privacy of our own pants. And the really sucky part is we're buying into it whether we realize it or not. Nearly everyone I talked to had no problem giving me jaw-droppingly graphic details of their girl-on-girl escapades, but when I asked them about masturbation they got all squirrely and clammed up. "That's just so girl," a friend of mine marveled, "we're so conditioned to make sure everyone around us is okay, to be good hostesses and all that, but when it comes to our own pleasures and needs they go second." Our whole masturbation situation is in sorry shape, and we seriously need to kick it up a notch. I'm not suggesting we start leering at men in movie theaters with our hands down our pants, but we need to start treating masturbation like the normal, healthy fun thing it is. Talk about it if we feel like talking about it. Do it when we feel like doing it. Give our daughters clearance to do it. Stop being ashamed of it.

There are a million reasons to masturbate and they're different for everybody. Most women masturbate to the point of orgasm, which some say relieves them of tension, stress, and menstrual cramps. Some say orgasms help them get to sleep, and others say they help them focus. Masturbating is also a great way to relieve pent-up sexual energy when there's no one to share it with. You can masturbate by yourself, over the phone, in a chat room, or in bed with a lover. Sometimes I masturbate just because I'm bored. Or tired and only kinda horny; I've woken up with my hand down there, job unfinished, many a time. It also comes in mighty handy when I've got writer's block—for some reason it settles me down and gets my creativity flowing.

> My hand is always in the mood and knows just how I like it. It's one of the best lovers I've ever had.
>
> —ANNIE, 33

Helping ourselves to ourselves also gives us a chance to figure out who we are and what we like in our own private learning environment, and that makes us more confident when we decide to share ourselves with another. In situations where this other turns out to be a member of the same sex, all the same benefits apply, along with some extra added bonuses. Not only can masturbation help you get over your inhibitions, but because you have the same equipment, if you know your way around yours you'll know your way around hers. As Carla, 32, said about her first experience with another woman: "I slid my hand down her pants and remember thinking 'Here we go!' I had no idea what I was doing! When I stuck my finger in her pussy it was like this wave went through me. It was a complete turn-on, so exciting and weird to feel something there just like what I had. I think I just went into autopilot, like I was fingering myself."

The many benefits of masturbation can be infinitely helpful in your quest to be a good lover to another woman. I've broken them down into three categories: "Mind," "Body," and "O."

Mind

A critical part of sleeping with other women is getting your head in the right space. If you've been existing solely in Boy World, it's a good idea to put a little energy into mentally shifting over to girls. Fantasizing while you masturbate is a great way to do that. If you can get yourself off by thinking about doing all sorts of nasty things to another woman (or three), you're more likely to get off when the real thing comes along. Take some time and let your imagination and your hands run free; don't resort to those shopworn old fantasies that get you to your quick fix. Keep in mind that fantasy is a place where anything goes, and that what you choose to do in your real life is a completely different story. Nobody ever has to find out how wild you are, so you can really have a field day. If thinking about getting gang-raped on the side of the freeway by a bunch of biker chicks gets you wet, that doesn't mean you really want it to happen. It also doesn't mean there's anything wrong with you. It just means you're a creative lady. So let your thoughts run free and start to focus on scenarios involving other women that really get you hot, whatever they may be.

Fantasy also comes in handy because it gives you a chance to be imaginative and map out ahead of time some ideas you might like to try. Heading off into unknown territory is much less intimidating when you have some idea what you're going to do once you get there. If you really hold yourself to a strict practice schedule and stay focused, I guarantee you'll work yourself into such a horned-out frenzy she won't know what hit her.

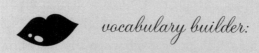 *vocabulary builder:*

FINGER FODDER:
the dirty little thoughts that help you masturbate.

A good way to get yourself turned on is by reading erotica, sexy novels, and watching movies in which hot chicks get it on. Not only can they get your juices flowing, but I find if I'm watching or reading something really good, it gives me the feeling I'm being let in on this great thing, like the women on the screen or on the page are participating in a world I want to be a part of. Some of my favorites are listed in the back of this book. In the meantime, here's a dirty little story to get your blood pumping:

shopping spree

Ever since Lindsay woke up from the dream she hadn't been able to get Catherine off her mind. Days had passed and the memory of that dream, of Catherine's long, powerful body pressed up against her own, still rushed through her system. It was as if this dream had not only enlightened her to the possibility of Catherine, but also awoke a strange and exciting part of herself.

Catherine owned a small used-clothing store at the bottom of Lindsay's street and Lindsay hardly knew her. She'd go in there every once in a while to see if anything new and interesting had come in and she and Catherine would chat about whatever. There was always something thick in the air between them but Lindsay had never given it much thought . . . before now. Now all of a sudden she was nervous about going to see her. She had

*no idea what she was going to do or whether Catherine
had any experience with women or what. All Lindsay
knew was that she had to see her or she'd go crazy.*

*When Lindsay walked into the store, Catherine was
standing on a ladder with her back to the door, hanging a
shirt on the wall. Her faded jeans sat low on her waist,
revealing the very top of her perfect ass and a tribal symbol tattooed on the small of her back. Her tight white
tank top pulled up away from her slender waist as she
raised her arms above her head to reach the nail. Lindsay stood beneath her and drank her in, taking advantage of the fact that she was unseen to notice the rush of
desire pulsing through her body.*

*Catherine slowly turned around, as if she sensed
Lindsay's presence. Lindsay held her breath, unable to
move or stop staring, worried that the heat rushing
through her had turned her cheeks bright red. Catherine
looked a little surprised at first, but instantly sensed
something different about Lindsay and returned her gaze
with a curious, mischievous stare. She descended the
ladder and turned to face Lindsay, her strong, lean arms
at her side, her lips slightly parted in an amused and
knowing grin. Neither one spoke, and as Catherine took
one confident step toward her, closing the gap between
them, Lindsay felt her stomach tighten and a pulse shoot*

straight to her crotch. "You're so sexy," she heard herself moan as Catherine leaned toward her and pressed her slender hand against Lindsay's burning cheeks. "And you're on fire," Catherine said, leaning down to press her full, hungry mouth to Lindsay's lips.

The sensation was unlike anything Lindsay had ever felt before, so soft and velvety that it seemed almost impossible, as if at any moment Catherine's mouth would somehow turn harder and become more like a man's. Lindsay was overcome with the need to know every curve of Catherine's body. She grabbed Catherine's ass with one hand, rubbing Catherine's crotch up against her own while she slid her other hand down the back of Catherine's jeans, along her perfect, round ass, past her panties and up into her hot, wet pussy. She slipped her finger deep inside Catherine and felt her own pussy throb with desire. It was warm and soft, just like her own, and as she slid her finger in and out she could almost feel it herself.

Catherine let out a moan and Lindsay gripped her tighter, pushing her tongue deep inside Catherine's mouth. She was so turned on that all her fear gave way to her wild desire to feel Catherine's soft, naked flesh against her own. In a breathless frenzy she removed Catherine's clothes and then her own. They lay down on

*the floor and Lindsay crawled on top of Catherine, feel-
ing her flesh melt into the pillow of softness beneath her.
She took Catherine's nipple in her mouth and sucked
hard, pressing her face down into her smooth porcelain
flesh. Impatient, she spread Catherine's legs, moved one
of her own between them, and pressed her hungry pussy
down hard against Catherine's clit. Catherine responded
by bucking her hips and grabbing Lindsay's ass, pressing
her down harder, greedily grinding their hungry clits together. Lindsay felt the orgasm inside her begin to build
and as she pressed down harder, Catherine slid her hand
around her ass and plunged two fingers deep inside
Lindsay's swollen pussy. She fucked her hard, pumping
her fingers in and out, gripping Lindsay's ass harder and
harder against her pussy. This was too much for Lindsay, who grabbed a handful of Catherine's hair and
pulled hard, grinding down harder and harder until she
could hold it in no more and exploded in orgasm.*

Body

Once you whet your mental appetite, it's safe to assume
your body will be ready to go—which will be hugely helpful because, as I pointed out, earlier, your own body is the
ultimate research library. You have the same equipment

and the luxury of really getting to know how it works in your own private, pressure-free learning environment before you take it on the road. Take some time and find all your hot spots. Figure out how hard or soft you like them touched—rub them, squeeze them, tickle them, tease them. It's possible she'll react the same way you do—if not, at least you'll be able to guide her when it comes to pleasing you. Play around with toys. Practice using a dildo or vibrator on yourself, get familiar with different sizes and speeds (see Chapter 6, "Pandora's Toybox," for details). If you find some toys that really do the trick, not only will your time at home alone improve but you'll also be motivated to get off your ass and find someone to enjoy them with. It's like when you're busting at the seams with any great idea: it's exciting to share. "I was lying on my stomach with my vibrator on my clit while I fucked myself with this dildo. I came so hard I almost put my head through the wall. Let me to do it to you!"

It's also fun to play with same-sex sex as if it were advanced masturbation, as if everything you're doing to her body you can feel on your own. For example, in one of my all-time favorite positions ever, she lies on her stomach and I crawl onto her back and lie on top of her, so that both our heads are facing down and my crotch is on top of her ass. Then I reach under and finger her the same way I'd finger myself. With my other hand I pull her hair or play with her breasts or finger her as well. This sends me through the roof, because I know I'm giving her pleasure, but since it's the same position I usually masturbate in, it seriously feels like I'm doing it to myself. It's like I'm masturbating but using her body instead. This is so hot I can't even tell you how hot it is.

Another thing: masturbation isn't always a solo activity. Once you get a lover, you can masturbate together, which is totally hot and very educational. You get to see what she does to herself to get off, so pay attention and surprise her with her own moves when you're in bed. You can also steal some of her more interesting moves that you might not have thought of and take them home for your own pleasure.

○

If you're sleeping with another woman, one of many goals will most likely be to get her to reach the Big O. As well as to get yourself to. By getting it on with yourself before hooking up with her, you can brush up on what makes you come, and maybe these same things will work for her. Discover all the different combinations of sensations and fantasies that get you to that point. Find out what gets you there the fastest, the slowest, not at all. Learn how to come without a man. Will you need to have a dildo on standby? Play around with controlling your orgasms. See how turned on you can get yourself and how long you can go without coming. Get yourself all the way to the breaking point and then pull away at the last second; repeat this until you can take it no more. Then maybe see how many times you can make yourself come in one round.

This is a great workout to get in shape for your foray into Girl Land, which you may need more than you'd expect because, as Jody, 37, pointed out: "When you're making love to a woman there's no beginning, middle, and end like there is with a guy. When he comes it's pretty much break time, whereas with a woman you can keep going and going and going for hours. . . . You could starve to death! I can't tell you how many times we've finally come up for air and realized that it's three in the morning and we're famished and all the restaurants are closed. I'll be found someday, dead in my bed, my skeleton knotted around hers."

This is not to say you can't bang out a quickie with another woman, but because we can come and keep going, sex can continue as long for as you want. And the better you know your own orgasm, the more fun you can have reining her in or letting her rip.

vocabulary builder:

Masturbation is such a stuffy, unsexy word (up there with "vagina" and "spinster"). Such a splendid pastime should have a name that does it justice. The following are some of my favorite female-specific terms for the Big M:

rolling the pebble
romancing the bean
calling Virginia
rubbing one out
scrubbing the cherry
stringing the love bead
double-clicking the mouse
auditioning the finger puppets
tickling the snail
paddling through poon lagoon
digging a trench

dousing the digits
drilling for oil
finger painting
paddling the pink canoe
parting the red sea
polishing the pearl
spelunking
shucking the oyster
morking the mindy
playing tag in the foxhole

Exploring your own body, like any other exploration, will be much more fruitful if you're familiar with the lay of the land. There's a lot going on out there, more than you may have realized, and knowing all your options could change the way you masturbate. Get in touch with your erogenous zones; notice which areas of your body are sensitive. Do certain smells or tastes get you horny? What dirty thoughts get you wet? Tug at your nipples and pull your hair. Run your fingers over your skin, tug at it, pinch it, tickle it. Notice how that feels. All of this will give you ideas as to what to do to her, and hopefully turn you on in the meantime.

The next section provides a no-holes-barred investigation into the clinical workings of the equipment in your nether regions. Even though I just urged you to explore your entire body, for now I'm only going to focus on what's between our legs. There will be a more comprehensive look at female erogenous zones in Chapter 4, "Gettin' Some 101."

Dr. Feelgood

If you've never seen what you look like down there, I highly recommend getting a hand mirror and checking yourself out. Unlike men who get an eyeful of their genitalia every time they take a piss, ours is tucked away and hidden from sight. Hooray—one more dopey reason women can be squirmy and weird about their sexuality! Knowledge is power, and the more familiar women are with their bodies, the more loving and fearless they'll be

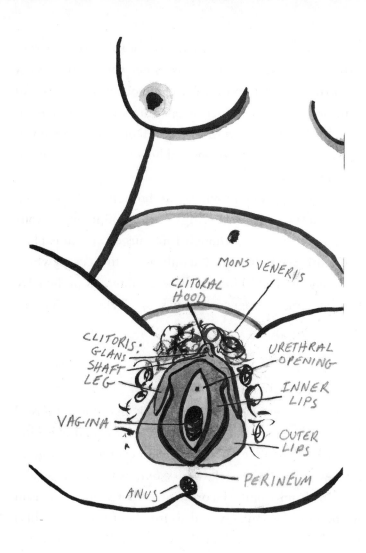

MONS VENERIS

CLITORAL HOOD

CLITORIS:
GLANS
SHAFT
LEG

URETHRAL OPENING

INNER LIPS

VAGINA

OUTER LIPS

PERINEUM

ANUS

FEMALE BUSINESS, FRONTAL VIEW

with themselves. It makes me sad to think about the number of people, my own granny included, who've never seen the underbelly of their own panty hamsters, who'd rather take a bullet than get busted squatting over a mirror. It's such a normal thing to be curious about, but I can guarantee that my nana's never treated herself to a peek. So, if you're reading this, Nana, even though your heart will have already stopped many pages ago, this illustration of a twat is dedicated to you.

Mons Veneris

This aptly named area (mons veneris is Latin for "hill of Venus") is most famous for the triangle of pubic hair that grows on it. The mons consists of fatty tissue that protects the pubic bone from the impact of sexual activity. In many women it's also a source of sexual pleasure.

Outer Lips (Labia Majora)

These cushy pads of fatty tissue are a continuation of the mons veneris and, like the mons, they sprout pubic hair. They contain sweat and oil glands that give off sexually arousing aromas. They also house many nerve endings and are a source of sexual pleasure.

Inner Lips (Labia Minora)

Full of nerve endings, the inner lips not only protect the vagina, urethra, and clitoris but they are also major receptors for sexual pleasure. They come in more sizes, shapes, and colors than you can imagine and are more sexually excitable than their sister outer lips.

Clitoris (glans, shaft, legs)

The clit is, hands down, the studliest part of the human body. Not only does its fabulous centerpiece, the glans, boast around eight thousand nerve endings in a teensy-weensy area, earning it the title of Most Sensitive Spot on the Human Body (the penis is rumored to have about four thousand spread out over a much larger area) but its *only* function is to provide pleasure. Period. No other body part in the wide world of body parts can say that about itself.

A common misconception is that the clit consists only of the glans, the tiny pearllike nub tucked beneath the clitoral hood (also known as your balloon knot). But the clit is much larger than what meets the eye. The glans sits atop the shaft, a half-inch-long-ish stem of erectile tissue that you may be able to feel if you rub yourself just above your glans when you're turned on. (Erectile tissue becomes engorged with blood when you're aroused.) The shaft then divides into two legs that spread out like a wishbone beneath the inner and outer lips, toward the sides of the vagina. The glans, shaft, and legs, as well as the area underneath the inner and outer lips, are all packed full of erectile tissue, making you all hot, swollen, and sensitive when you're ready to get it on.

Clitoral Hood

This layer of skin is analogous to the foreskin on a penis. It serves to protect the highly sensitive jewellike glans nestled in its flaps, and to mute some of the sensations it receives (given those eight thousand nerve endings, touching the clit directly can sometimes be painful).

Vagina

Heralded as the primary female pleasure spot pretty much up until the women's movement, the vagina was knocked out of first place by the clitoris when some people who actually gave a hoot about female sexual pleasure started doing a little research on the topic. It was always assumed that since when you stick yer dick in thar it feels real good, it must feel good for her, too. This is true, but many women can't orgasm without also stimulating the clitoris, which is not part of the vagina.

Still, the happy hole loves attention, and vaginal stimulation and penetration remain at the top of the charts. The majority of pleasurable nerve endings in the vagina are right around the opening and the area about two inches inside. The vagina also scores points because it provides access to the G-spot, a wildly popular area in most women. The vagina is also where the majority of your natural lubrication is produced, another very important contribution to your sexual pleasure.

Vaginal note: Keep in mind that getting wet doesn't always mean you're turned on, and sometimes you can be turned on and be totally dry. All sorts of things like moods, drugs, stress, and where you are in your cycle can affect how wet or dry you are, so it's good to keep some lube on hand in case your girl is taking the day off.

G-spot

The G-spot first came on the scene much the same way the Loch Ness Monster did. It was this mysterious thing that everyone was talking about, people went searching for, and the lucky few who had sightings reported back with blurry pictures and confusing details. Today there are countless books and websites on the topic, complete with diagrams and maps on how to get there.

vocabulary builder

A rose by any other name is still a rose, but at least it never had to be called "Vagina." Here are some creative monikers for the pretty kitty:

panty hamster	*pussy*
hoo	*batcave*
good girl	*bearded lady*
poonany	*cootch*
quim	*cunny*
muff	*love jungle*
hush puppy	*nooch*
hooch	*snatch*
loo loo	*wadge*
cherry pop	*cunt*
chuff	*yoni*
furry monkey	*volvo*

The G-spot is a section of spongy erectile tissue that surrounds the urethra and can be felt through the front wall of the vagina. It's formed from the same tissue as the prostate is in men, and it can give intense sexual pleasure if pressed or massaged. The best way to find it (which can be a little tricky) is to get really turned on first, so all the G-spot's erectile tissue fills with blood and makes it bigger. Stick your finger inside yourself and bend it forward, toward your belly button. You should feel a patch that sticks out a bit from the surrounding area—it's spongier, too, and maybe a little more textured. G-spots vary in size and location, but in general that's where you should be able to find yours. Likewise, everyone can react differently to having it stimulated. Some women go crazy with pleasure, some find it uncomfortable, and I personally feel nothing at all. I've spent hours upon hours poking around up there; rubbing the spongy sticky-outy part, and have felt nothing.

There are also times when G-spot stimulation can make you feel like you really have to pee, since the spot is so close to the bladder. If this keeps you from enjoying yourself, make sure to go to the bathroom beforehand and then try to relax—it's normal to feel like pee is on the way, but it's not.

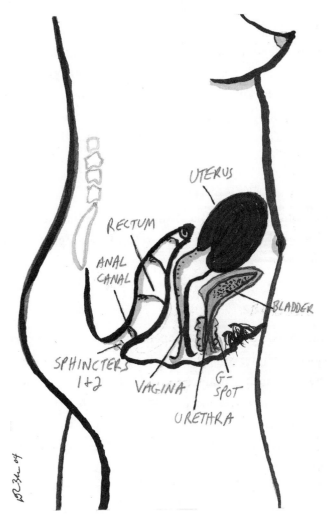

FEMALE BUSINESS, SIDE VIEW

Perineum

Fondly referred to as your taint ('tain't yer vagina, 'tain't yer asshole), the perineum is the area between your vagina and your anus. Beneath the surface is the perineal sponge, which is made up of sensitive erectile tissue that swells when you're aroused and feels mighty fine when touched.

Urethra

A two-inchish tube that runs from your bladder to your pee hole (also known as your urethral opening).

Anus, Anal Canal, Sphincter 1 and Sphincter 2, Rectum

Your anus, the puckered opening to your anal canal, is loaded with nerve endings, erectile tissue, and blood vessels, making it a major contender in the sexual pleasure arena. Licking, vibrating, stroking, poking are all yummy treats for the brown spider.

Directly inside the anus are your tight little sphincter muscles. The first one you come to, the exterior sphincter, is the one you'd tense up to hold in your poop or gas. Your internal sphincter, which is directly behind it, is controlled by your autonomic nervous system and, like your heartbeat, works without your thinking about it. I mention these not because they give you sexual pleasure, but because if you're going to receive sexual pleasure through anal penetration, relaxing these muscles is a must. Deep breathing, trust, practice, and lots and lots of lube will get you there.

After the sphincter muscles comes the anal canal (the area just inside the anus) which is made up of sensitive erectile tissue. The anal canal leads to your rectum, which is also made up of erectile tissue and which, like your anal canal, loves the feeling of being pressed and massaged. Because your G-spot is located behind your anal canal (much like the prostate gland is in men), if you get in the right position you can press up against it during anal penetration, which can feel pretty damn excellent. If the whole poop thing skeeves you out too much, know that it may not play as big a part in butt fun as you may think. Poop is stored in your colon—which is way at the tippy top and really hard to reach—not in your anal canal or rectum.

Now that you've had a brief tour of the South, we can move on to the fun part.

When I need a quick fix I lie on top of my hands and grind until I come. Sometimes I sniff a pair of my own panties while I'm at it—the smell really turns me on.

—KATIE, 18

How to Do You

There is no right way or wrong way to masturbate. Pretty much anything you do that gives you any sort of sexual pleasure counts, and what feels good can be different for different people. Some women like to lie on their stomachs, some stand; some use vibrators, some hate 'em; some women need visual stimulation, some find it distracting. I usually need some raunchy mental input to go along with all my stroking and rubbing, but plenty of women I spoke to don't use fantasies at all. Focusing on the physical pleasure they're giving themselves is all they need to get off. Likewise, you can masturbate to the point of orgasm, or you can luxuriate in the journey, or both. It's all about you and what you want, with no outside pressure at all.

Think of it as spending some quality time with your body, this utterly incredible machine that most of us take for granted most of the time. I mean, how often do you stop to think about the fact that your heart is beating, *al-*

ways, or that you're constantly regenerating cells, or that you can walk, see, bend your finger, or that you even have a finger? The more in touch you are with your body, the more grounded, self-aware, and awestruck you'll be. Masturbation is the most intimate way to physically check in and appreciate some of the great things your body can do for you—especially if you keep in mind that there's a lot more to it than just playing with your genitals. Your body is riddled with erogenous zones, and infinite amounts of pleasure can be derived from touching them. When's the last time you appreciated how soft your skin is, or how exciting it is to run your own tongue over your lips? You also have smell, sight, sound, and taste to add to the mix. Maybe the smell of a lover's T-shirt or a picture of two women fingering each other can enhance your experience. I highly recommend you explore all your options: it'll not only bring you a ton of pleasure but also help you be a more creative lover with the ladies, since everything you do to yourself can be done to her as well.

The following are just a few of the many, many ways women masturbate. I hope they'll inspire you, turn you on, and/or teach you something you didn't know before. I was blown away by a lot of the stuff I read and was inspired to try it out myself (making this chapter the one that took me the longest to write). Keep in mind that I'm only describing the especially fun hot things that people do, I'm not bothering with "I rolled over onto my hand in the middle of the night, rubbed, came, passed out"—that's common enough but doesn't make for a very interesting read or offer much inspiration. So don't think that all these women are out there swinging from the rafters, giving themselves these rowdy orgasms night after night—they're not. When people write in or talk to me about sex they're only giving the highlights (and no doubt spicing them up a bit). So don't feel like you're missing out on something or that you're a sexual bore because nobody out there is walking away with the gold medal every single time.

> I love rubbing myself while I'm driving. One time I drove alongside this trucker—I pretended I didn't see him, but knowing he was watching was such a turn on.
>
> —PATTY, 54

The Joy of Fingering

This is one of the best, most hassle-free ways to get yourself off. You don't have to drag out any toy boxes, climb into any bathtubs, find batteries for any vibrators . . . you can just get right down to business. Your fingers are incredibly versatile, nimble tools that can bring you pleasure in infinite ways. Not only can they experience touch themselves, but you can completely control how fast, slow, hard, or soft they do their work. Here are some of my favorite things to do with my fingers:

- Lie on your back and spread your legs wide. Softly run your hands over your whole body. Tickle your arms, caress your tits, pinch your nipples, draw a slow line from your throat down to your pussy. Slowly run your finger from the opening of your vagina up to your clit. Repeat this over and over, teasing yourself by doing it very softly while you fantasize. If you're dry, add some lube to your finger.
- Grab your clit between your thumb and forefinger and gently roll it back and forth. Squeeze it and tug on it, tickle it and tap it.
- Pull the hair on the back of your head while you push two fingers into your vagina, pressing down on your clit with the palm of your hand. Rub your palm around in slow, firm circles and increase the speed as you get more turned on.
- Lie on your stomach with your hand over your pussy, using your body weight to grind into your hand. Wiggle your fingers inside your vagina while

pressing down hard. Push them in and out, pumping harder and harder. Concentrate on the feeling and whatever fantasy you're into.

🍒 Lick your finger and slowly rub it along your lips (the ones on your mouth). Feel the sensation while you caress your clit with your other hand. Slip your finger inside your mouth and suck on it while you penetrate your vagina with your other hand.

Here are some suggestions from other fans of the finger:

I like to look at pictures of men fucking women. I get naked on my bed and pretend that I'm the girl in the picture and that the man with the rock-hard cock who's staring down at her is staring down at me. I rub the skin on my belly and my arms and imagine he's the one doing it while he strokes his dick. I pretend he's licking me all over my body, making me beg to get fucked. I stop touching myself completely and torture myself, imagining him staring hungrily down at me, his huge throbbing cock in his hand. He makes me beg for it, teases me by barely putting it in while I stick my fingers inside myself a tiny bit. When I can't take it anymore I let myself have it, pounding away until I come.

–Karen, 37

I slowly take off my pants and panties, I feel them slide off my skin and start tingling with excitement since I know what's about to come! I kneel on my bed and remove my shirt and bra slowly, pretending I'm a stripper, while I grind my hips in anticipation. I fling my hair around, squeezing my tits hard and grinding my hips. I put some lube on the fingers of my right hand and lie down, grabbing my bedpost with the other. I start rubbing on my clit in a circular motion as I pull hard on the bedpost. I pretend I'm tied to the bed as I pull harder and fantasize about a sexy woman sucking on my clit and licking my whole pussy. I pretend I can't get untied. Then I slide my thumb sideways along my clit, grinding it in a circular motion while I stick my middle finger up my ass. This drives me wild and I have to make myself come! I take my hand from the bedpost and stick two fingers into my pussy while I pump my asshole with the middle finger of my other hand. I roll over onto my stomach and send my fingers in deep and feel my whole body quiver and shake with an incredible orgasm!

—Hilary, 49

Water

Playing with water is one of the biggest crowd-pleasers I've come across. Women who've never masturbated before or who have trouble getting themselves off especially love it. Water running over a clitoris brings such an incredible amount of pleasure that it sends some previously unmoved women through the roof. If you're having trouble grasping this whole masturbation thing, I urge you to give water a whirl. And if you're a seasoned pro, you may want to add some of these to your repertoire:

I start by lighting all the candles in my bathroom. I turn on the bathtub, get the water the perfect temperature (lukewarm) and slide in with my pussy right beneath the faucet, putting my legs on the wall. I let the water spill all over my pussy, move myself from side to side and let it flow inside me and wash over my clit. I lie back in the tub and squeeze my nipples until I come so hard I scream!

–Jenna, 24

MASTURBATING IN THE BATHTUB

I don't know who invented the removable showerhead, but it had to be a woman! I got one that has a massaging head that lets you adjust the amount of water that comes out—from tiny streams to gushing rivers. You can also adjust the pressure of the water and put it on pulse (yum!) I just stand in the shower and play around with the water pressure. I usually begin with my nipples, ro-

tating the tiny pins of water around and around, making my whole body tingle. Then I slowly move the shower-head down between my legs and spray it back and forth from my clit to my anus. This is usually where the pulse part comes in! I move it back and forth between my legs, letting the water hammer away at me until I come. There is nothing on earth like it!

—Alyson, 36

When I was a teenager, I discovered the secret joys of the Shower Massage. Up until then I didn't even know what an orgasm was. Or what a clit was. Once I got that thing battering my naive little clit, I was racking violently from spasms of pleasure almost instantly. I mean instantly. I could make my orgasms last as long as I could take it.

—Michelle, 41

If you're in the bathtub, another variation is to get on all fours and back up to the faucet, getting as low as you need to to get the water to run over your pussy. And those of you who don't have a removable showerhead can try lying down in the tub with the shower on and let the water spray onto your pussy. While you're at it, take an empty shampoo bottle and squeeze it onto your nipples.

The suction feels great. You can also use an empty bottle to fill up with water and squirt onto your clit. Also recommended are water jets in jacuzzis and pools. Just slide your crotch in front of the jet stream and hold on, being careful not to get too close if the water is coming out too fast.

Humping and Grinding

The excellent thing about humping (besides the word itself) is that you can use your body weight to really get in there and grind away. Rubbing your clit up against anything that'll stand still long enough—pillows, table corners, stuffed animals, door knobs, banisters, fellow human beings—will do the trick. You can control how hard or how soft you want the friction to be, and you can combine your humping with fingering yourself or using a vibrator or whatever. Here are some techniques that might work for you.

I stack up a bunch of pillows in the middle of my bed and straddle them. I squeeze them with my thighs and grind my pussy into them, rocking back and forth, thrusting and grinding down as hard and fast as I can. Sometimes I drop onto all fours and reach back and spank myself. I also love to watch my ass in the mirror while I grind. It's so naughty!

—Zoe, 18

I just upgraded my stereo system and got some new speakers. Each speaker has the regular speaker part and then a separate box called a sub woofer that most of the bass comes out of. And let me tell you honey, they could sell these things to women all the time if they'd let us sit on them at the store! I usually start by putting on a flimsy nighty and pouring myself a cocktail. Then I put on some hip-hop or R&B, something sexy with a fat bassline, turn it up nice and loud and sit myself down on the speaker. I wiggle around, letting my clit hit the hard smooth wood and bam—I'm done before the song is!

—Kimberly, 48

I love shaving my pussy. Having a freshly shaved pussy makes me ten times more sensitive, I can feel every little thing I brush up against to the point where I'm so wet all the time I have to masturbate at least four or five times a day! Luckily I have a door that locks at work, and one of my favorite things to do is fuck my chair. I know this sounds weird, but it feels fantastic. It's one of those big, black, cushioned chairs on wheels. The arms are padded and fairly narrow, the perfect size for my starving pussy. I kneel on the seat of the chair with one leg and straddle the arm, leaving my other foot on the ground. Then I start rubbing, hugging the back of the chair with both arms and grinding my pussy back and forth, rubbing my tits against the back of the chair. I grip the back harder and harder and grind away, thinking about my sweet swollen pink pussy the whole time.

–Rachel, 39

Toys, Etc.

Sex toys can take masturbating to a whole new level—if you can rub your clit so fast your teeth chatter, a vibrator can do it faster. And however deeply you can finger-fuck yourself, a dildo can go deeper. Yet this doesn't necessarily mean sex toys are for everyone. Plenty of women aren't the least bit excited by them; plenty of others would brave a blizzard to get to the store because their dog ate their butt plug. There are so many different sizes and shapes and purposes that shopping for toys can be a bit overwhelming; before you head out, see Chapter 6, "Pandora's Toybox: Advanced Gettin' Some." Also, be diligent about keeping your toys clean. The best way is to use a condom on anything you stick inside yourself, which may seem weird when you're all alone, but it can prevent you from getting a yeast infection or other unwanted nastiness.

If you like the idea of playing with toys, here are some ideas to inspire you:

I like to lie on my stomach with my bullet vibrator on pulse under my clit while I slide a large Sharpie in and out of my ass. Mmmmmmm.

–Pamela, 29

I'm addicted to getting fucked in chat rooms. I don't care if it's a man or a woman–if they can talk dirty, bring 'em on! I've got it down to a science: I sit at my computer naked with my dildo on the chair underneath my snatch so I can grind away on it. It's all about being able to get off and still being able to type. I sometimes also use my trusty vibrator (a long, dick-shaped one) and put the head on my clit and the other end against the bottom of my desk. It fits perfectly and stays put, and it's the most incredible combo!

–Janine, 52

I'm pretty new to masturbating and have only used my hand, but the other night I made an amazing discovery. I came home kind of drunk and so horny I couldn't wait to masturbate. For some reason my usual fingering of my clit and vagina wasn't enough—I felt like I needed more—so I ran around my house looking for something to stick inside myself and found a banana! It wasn't very ripe, so it was hard, and it was curved perfectly. I put a condom on it because I was scared it would break open inside me. I couldn't believe how great it felt—I highly recommend trying this!

—Kara, 18

I've had plenty of boyfriends and a very active sex life, but I didn't have an orgasm until last year. When I finally did I was like, Oh my God, so this is an orgasm! I finally realized it wasn't penetration but clitoral stimulation that did it for me. All I can say is there's this thing called the Oscillator. It's like a hundred bucks and has three differ-ent levels of vibration: slow, medium, and fast. It's the greatest gift I've ever given myself. I just lie on my back, stick it on my clit, hit the switch, and I'm off! And then if I use it with a dildo I have the greatest orgasm I've ever had. Sometimes I take the express bus home because I can't wait to get there and masturbate.

—Carolee, 46

When it comes to finding devices to get yourself off, your options are pretty much endless. Not only has the sex industry provided a mind-numbing array of toys and aides, but depending on how creative and resourceful you are, there's no end to the innocent household objects that can be converted into tools of desire. Here's a brief list of items that have been reported to lead double lives:

Hairbrushes
Plier handles
Electric toothbrushes
Pens
Ringing phones
Electric razors
Cucumbers
Carrots
Eggplants
Ice cubes
Candlesticks
Pot handles
Vacuum cleaners
Broom handles
Stuffed animals
Pool cues
Spoons

Once you get into it, you'll never view a trip to the hardware store the same way.

safety first!

What goes up your ass does not go in your vagina! This means fingers, toys, shampoo bottles, everything must be cleaned before switching holes. The bacteria found up your butt can be incredibly damaging to your sweet pussy. And fer fuck's sake, don't use anything breakable or anything that can get stuck up there. There's nothing sexy about going to the emergency room.

Look Ma, No Hands!

I can't remember how or when I discovered I could bring myself to orgasm without using my hands, but it's forever changed the way I view long, boring meetings, plane trips, weddings, and waiting for my number to be called at the DMV. Because you don't use your hands or get a tell-tale boner, once you get the system down you can get away with sneaking a little treat any old time you want—especially if you can keep yourself from moaning and thrashing, which can be a bit of a challenge. If you're pretty new to the masturbation game, this method may be too advanced, so don't get discouraged if you try it and it does nothing for you. Most people have to work up to it, even those of you who get yourselves off all the time. But once you figure it out, it's awesome, and you can mess around with a bunch of different variations. All you need is unflinching concentration, a little squeezing of some muscles down there, and a whore's chest full of filthy thoughts. Here's what you do.

- Sit with your legs crossed. For me, it works best to have them stretched out in front of me, crossed at the ankles.

- Squeeze your inner thighs together, clench your butt cheeks, and tighten your stomach muscles. Flex and release your upper inner-thigh muscles. Keep flexing and releasing, and take little breaks if it gets to be too much—you're clenching a whole bunch of muscles and you don't want to pull anything.

- Fantasize about the most graphic, hottest, filthiest thing you can think of. This is the most important part, because you're getting so little physical stimulation you'll need to rely mostly on your mind to get you where you're going. It helps to do this part first, get yourself all worked up and horny as hell, and then slide into position. Concentration is key, so you can't really do this in a situation where anyone's expecting you to speak or interact in any way. Keep the fantasy strong and in the very front of your mind, and as your excitement builds, flex and release your upper thigh muscles. As you build toward climax, focusing hard on that fantasy, keep your muscles flexing tighter and tighter. You'll feel your face getting red (I usually keep my head down or hide behind a magazine), your heart rate quicken, and then (I hope!) the flush of an orgasm.

Variations

🍒 Sit with your legs crossed at the thighs, slouched over a bit, with your butt cheeks clenched and pulled tightly beneath you. I find this one of the more difficult positions, but when crammed into a movie theater seat or a lecture hall chair, a girl doesn't have much option to stretch out. Again, it's all about flexing those thigh/groin muscles and concentrating on your fantasy.

🍒 Lie on your stomach, legs stretched out, butt cheeks

clenched, pubic bone pressing into the ground. I've worked this one poolside many a time. If you do happen to be outside in a bathing suit, it's nice to start out on your back and let the hot sun warm up your pussy. There's something about heating her up that always gets me in the mood.

Tips

In general, it's important to think about how you can hide your face if you're somewhere people can see you. Chances are very good you're going to go beet red and look like you're about to explode. Newspapers, magazines, books, hooded sweatshirts, and staring at your lap can all help with this. I also recommend wearing tight pants since it gives your clit something to press against. And concentrate on your fantasy. I can't stress that enough.

chapter three

Obtaining a Visitor's Pass

It wasn't like I looked at her and she was really hot, it was more like we were hanging out and then it just happened. It kind of came out of nowhere.

—MELISSA, 43

You've finally decided to go for it—now what the hell do you do? Depending on where you live and what you're looking for, there are tons of different ways to find a girl to sleep with. In general, picking up chicks really isn't all that different from picking up guys. Most of the same stuff is involved: trying to be witty, sucking, being rejected, trying again, victory, butterflies, self-doubt, beer goggles, etc.

Luckily, the laws of the heterosexual dating jungle have been much amended in the past several decades, so most women are used to being aggressive. It's no longer up to the boys to pick up a dropped hankie, and many a marriage has come to pass because she, not he, got down on bended knee. I myself have informed more than one lucky guy that I'm available for dinner. I've even paid, walked him home, and begged him to let me come upstairs and look at the baseball card collection he's been bragging about all night. Likewise, the rules are pretty open in the girl world, so it's up to you how you want to play it. You can either bat your eyes and play hard to get, or saddle up and ask her something suave like "Are those space pants you're wearing? 'Cuz your ass is out of this world."

Perhaps it's time to invite your old college roommate over for martinis followed by a surprise bubble bath? Or you might set out on a shopping spree with your boyfriend, in search of the perfect third. Or maybe you'd like to try getting a lesbian sponsor. If you're hot, and you alert your local gay community, chances are very good you can find a real live lesbian to ease your passage into bisexuality.

sleeping with chicks tip #2:

Lesbians are into women. If you're just experimenting, don't be a dickhead and use her for sex when you can tell she has feelings for you.

However you go about it, I highly recommend being as prepared as possible. As in any new situation, you have a much better chance of being successful if you show up with your homework done. You wouldn't hit a sample sale without a credit card and a stun gun, nor should you make your foray to the other side of sex without a few key items.

The Straight Girl's Starter Kit

Nail Clippers

Think about it. The pussy is a very sensitive lady. Going at her with long fingernails is about as sexy as going at her with a rake. Showing up untrimmed will not only broadcast your inexperience but may also genuinely terrify potential dates. There are people who will insist that this is b.s., and I know there are women who can type with full-on swords growing out of their fingertips. But it's a skill that goes against all the physical laws of nature. I don't trust it. In fact, if anyone came at me with claws like that, I think I'd make her take a typing test before I let her anywhere near my unmentionables.

A Two-Track Mind

It's possible that you're so used to dealing with men that you're oblivious to signs being flung at you by the ladies. You need to consciously open your mind and start taking in information from places you haven't before. Pay attention to how women talk to you. Is she saying "That's a really cute shirt you have on," or "That's a *really* cute shirt you have on"? You could be getting hit on left and right and not even know it.

Likewise, you need to start sending out your own sparks in a more womanly direction. Train your mind to think of women as possible bedmates. We're always checking each other out anyway, looking at how she wears her hair or trying to figure out where she got those pants. It's time to start trying to figure out what's inside those pants. Once you do, you'll realize how often it happens to you. It's like when your friend says she just got a Jack Russell Terrier. You've never heard of the things, and you don't really like dogs anyway, but you agree to meet her dog and all of a sudden you see them all over the place. It's not because there's suddenly been a locust swarm of Jack Russell Terriers, it's because you've opened your consciousness to them and now you're seeing what's been around you the whole time. It sounds really hippie-dippie but I swear it's true.

A Flask and a One-Hitter

If you have the pre-girl jitters, there's nothing wrong with relying on a little help from your friends. Sometimes a little social lubricant can be the difference between striking up a conversation with a sexy stranger and running home to Mommy. Mind-altering substances also serve as excellent lures for getting the ladies to follow you somewhere where you can be alone. Buying Sheila a drink is fine, but why not wow her with your own private bar behind the dumpster in the parking lot? A flask and a one-hitter can be your own secret weapons, just like sexy undies: even if you never show them off, just knowing they're there sometimes provides you all the confidence you need.

A New Relationship with Your Wardrobe

One of the cool things about hooking up with women is that it gives you a different sense of yourself. You may find that you begin to dress differently, or you carry yourself differently in the clothes you already have. It's like you've suddenly been handed this new doll and you get to figure out how she walks and what she wears. Think about how you want to feel with another chick—do you want to be all pretty and girly or do you want to play around with your masculine side?

In the lesbian world this is a big deal. Presenting yourself as femme or butch is viewed as claiming your role in a relationship and society in general. A common complaint I get from a lot of my lesbian friends is that they feel incredible pressure to define themselves as one or the other when most of them just feel like "I'm a woman who likes to be with other women; who gives a shit if I'm femme or butch?" But for us straighties, waffling back and forth from our masculine to our feminine side is no biggie, more just a fun thing we can play around with.

Even the slightest change in what you're wearing, or your attitude toward what you're wearing, can be such a turn-on. For example, if you have a pair of biker boots that you wear all the time, when you start going for chicks you might strut in them differently. You may feel more turned on by the fact that they make you feel kind of masculine in a way that attracts chicks, not just in a way that makes you feel tough. It's very subtle, but it's totally hot.

Think about what you're wearing and start to see yourself as a hottie through feminine eyes. Think about what turns you on about other women and accentuate that part of yourself. Go through your closet and think "Hmmm, what would *she* think of this?" rather than "What would he . . . ?" Think of yourself as someone who sleeps with chicks while you're getting dressed and walking around and I swear you'll notice a difference.

Local Lesbian Zines and Newspapers

If you live somewhere with any kind of self-respecting gay scene, there should be some publications that address lesbian issues and list the lesbian goings-on about town. Get a hold of some of these and check out where the lesbo bars are, peruse the personals, read your gay horoscope. I realize that this may seem mighty gay to the merely curious, but sometimes it's best to go straight to the source. Your chances of scoring are higher, since the women you'll meet are most likely into chicks. This way if you shoot and miss, it's just because they thought you sucked, not because they're not into sleeping with women.

These publications are also good for reading up on current events and women's issues. Knowledge is sexy and it can up your appeal. You can learn which concert T-shirts are the real head-turners with the ladies, or jump in on a conversation about the present state of women's health issues. Lesbian magazines, such as *Curve* and *Girlfriends*, can also be useful as sex flares—carry them around under your arm, covers facing out, and alert all who pass that you're game.

This said, I feel the need to fly a couple of red flags here. Seeking out chicks at a lesbian bar can be a little intimidating. It's sort of like picking up guys at a sports bar—you're totally on their turf and you could be treated as an outsider, meaning you'll either be ignored or catch some hostility. I highly doubt anything really horrible will happen to you, but as anyone who's ever walked into a bar and had it go silent knows, it's not really very fun. Another possibility is that someone might think you're hot and, being on their turf and all, will feel completely comfortable hitting on you with the force of a wrecking ball. The most likely possibility, however, is that you'll have just as much fun as you do in any ol' bar and it'll be no big deal at all.

As far as the magazines go, there's a slight chance that an innocent flip-through will curdle your curiosity for good. At the risk of having the entire lesbian population gather outside my house with baseball bats, I will now ever so lightly address the issue of the aesthetics in the publications I've checked out. And I think all I'm going to say is they could use a little sprucing up. *In general.* I've seen a bunch that get good photographers and take hot pictures using attractive models. But I've also seen a buttload that haven't—a lot of what I've seen out there will have you running out to marry the first guy who asks you. Who decided that taking photos of unattractive women in unflattering outfits under fluorescent lighting was a good idea? And where are all the models who look like the hot lesbians I know? I know that they're not publishing this stuff for a straight girl like me, so I'm sure they could give a rat's ass what I think, but I just wanted those of you who've experienced similar reactions to know you're not alone. And to encourage you to forage through anyway. Whether or not you find the eye candy in these magazines appealing, they can be very informative and worth checking out.

Finger Condoms and Latex Dams

Different equipment, different protection, same reasons. After reading Chapter 4, "Gettin' Some 101," you'll more fully understand how they're useful and in what acts, but the subject of protection can never be brought up too early. Any good sex shop in town will carry everything you need. And if you live in the boonies, there are plenty of places online that would love to take your money. In the straight world, sticking a raincoat on Mr. Happy is about protecting him from you as much as it is about protecting yourself from him. Bodily fluids of both sexes are potentially deadly and you're just as much of a pinhead if you hook up with chicks unprotected as you are if you have unprotected sex with men. Yes, it's harder to get HIV from a woman, but it's far from impossible, and there's a host of other diseases that would just love to hop on and take you for a ride.

It seems to me like the American public deals with diseases as if they were fads, like they're only worth talking about when they're new and mysterious. Once their fifteen minutes of fame are up, our A.D.D. is captured by the latest scary discovery and we brush our old fears under the rug with last year's fashions. AIDS? That was like, so eighties. Herpes and syphilis? Jesus, who invited them? But they're all alive and well and a major part of more and more lives every year, front-page news or not. It's up to you to keep on top of things regardless of where the media's spotlights are pointed. And showing up with the proper protection separates you from the apes.

If you're sleeping with women you'll need finger condoms and latex dams. Finger condoms are little tubes you slide over your fingers that protect any cuts you may not be aware of. Chances are excellent that if you're fooling around with a woman your fingers will wind up in contact with a fluid or two at some point. If you have a cut and she has something gnarly, you will never forgive yourself. Likewise, latex dams will protect your precious mouth and pussy from suffering the same fate. Latex dams are just a super-thin layer of latex that you slip between you and her before it gets hot and heavy. Not as hot as skin on skin but really not so bad: these things are made with sex in mind, so the creators have taken your tactile pleasure into consideration. They're not making them with recycled tire rubber or anything. You barely know they're there—and even if you do know, they sure beat the hell out of dropping dead or having fire ants take over your crotch.

Come Out, Come Out, Wherever You Are

Where does someone interested in sleeping with another chick find this other chick? I think it's safe to say that whatever scenario you're comfiest meeting men in will be your best bet when it comes to meeting women. If you're not comfortable, it's hard to do anything, especially be confident and sexy and flirty. I've met the majority of my boyfriends through mutual friends. The only man I ever picked up in a bar was so drunk I left him on a bench halfway home, and hell would surely freeze over if I ever sat on a plane next to a hot guy, or even one who's remotely attractive, single, and interested. Left to my own devices, I might never exchange a bodily fluid again. Especially should I find myself attempting to navigate foreign terrain, the kind with boobs and curves and stuff.

So in general, I say sticking with the tried and true is best if possible. But since you may be looking for something different in your same-sex mate—a third, or a quick fling—the tried and true may not apply. If you met your boyfriend through friends of your parents, for example, you probably don't want to put the word out to Mom and Dad that you're looking for someone to suck his balls while you make out with him. You may have to step outside your usual routine, but despair not. Your options are many and varied and discussed below.

> I always have great luck in strip clubs—strippers are the best! They're up for anything.
>
> —ELIZABETH, 23

vocabulary builder

A LICKETY SPLIT:
a one-night stand with a chick

I'd like to point out a special bonus prize that the straight-girl population might not be aware of. Because you're a chick dealing with other chicks, you have the Curious Straight Girl's All-Access Backstage Pass. You automatically gain entry to saunas, group showers, dressing rooms, and a host of other intimate settings where women are not only off their guard, but naked! You have a coveted VIP pass. Don't waste it. Think about all the situations you could get yourself into that would make sleeping with a chick a snap:

- Host a slumber party/kegger at your sorority house, complete with beer bong and group sleeping area
- Get a game of Twister going at your next pool party
- Suggest that the bride-to-be model all her new lingerie at your next bridal shower
- Take pole-dancing lessons with your hot friends
- Hire a female stripper at your next bachelorette party
- Play Truth or Dare with your friends in a hot tub
- Ask for help unzipping your dress in the locker room
- Get a bikini wax from a hot chick
- Instigate a game of spin the bottle at your next girls' night out

SPIN THE BOTTLE

There are so many straight women that you can have if you want. Just find somebody cute, flatter her, tell her what's honestly beautiful about her, and she'll be into it. As a woman, you really know what other women like to hear.

—JEANNIE, 29

Sometimes the best way to get ideas for what would work for you is by pulling from other people's experiences. Here's how it happened for some of the people I spoke to:

Dramatic Reenactments
of Actual Women Hooking Up

At a Wedding

I was a bridesmaid in my best friend's wedding and I wound up fooling around with another bridesmaid in the back of the limo. Always a bridesmaid, never a bride! She was bi and we went to high school together but I never really considered sleeping with her, or any girl for that matter. But we had the limo to ourselves and one minute she was making me laugh and the next minute she had her face in my crotch. It was really hot, actually. It must have looked pretty ridiculous, two giant pink pastries getting it on. I spent the night in her room and took the walk of shame back to mine the next morning.

–Julie, 23

On a Date

I was on this really bad double date with a friend of mine. We were both miserable so we decided to get really wasted. We were all sitting at the bar and the guys were trying their best but we wanted none of it. We decided to start making out to get them to leave us alone and I nearly fell over. I had no idea it would be that electric! We ended up ditching them and going back to her place, where we fooled around all night.

–Kathleen, 34

On the Road

I went to college in Chicago and used to catch a ride home to New York at the end of the year with this girl named Molly. We would usually do it straight through, switching off driving while the other slept, but one year we got stuck in Ohio and had to get a room for the night. We were lying there in the dark in the big king-sized bed, and we somehow got on the topic of sex. We started telling it all in graphic detail, cracking up and stuff, and I was pretty worked up by the time she told me she'd been with a woman. It wasn't like she was coming on to me or anything, she was just describing what she'd done, and I had so many questions I guess I let on that I was really curious. Pretty soon I felt her hand on my thigh and I just went for it. I leaned over to kiss her, and I remember a little voice screaming in my head, "Oh my god, here I go!" That night always comes up now whenever I talk about sex!

–Maya, 30

In the Dentist's Chair

I was still married, but my husband was about to move out when I met her. She was my dentist, really cute, vivacious, hip, attractive. Very full of vitality, which I felt I was lacking at that time—I was in this humdrum relationship that I was trying to end. I invited her to lunch and there was all this sexual tension. I had been attracted to women in the past, but usually they were straight. I'd never been attracted to a lesbian. The first time we kissed was a week or so later at her house. She said she wanted to kiss me but felt awkward, so I kissed her. It felt really great—soft, interesting, and sexual. I was attracted to her as a person as opposed to just thinking this might be fun. I still consider myself straight even though we fell madly in love and were together for eight months.

—Carrie, 41

In the Coat Check

I was at a bar and there was this hottie girl there. A straight girl, straighty straight looked so straight and she was with this guy and another girlfriend of hers. They went up to the bar at the same as I did, I said something funny, we started talking, they bought me shots, etc. So we talked and talked and the whole night she was joking "You know we should get married, we have so much in common." Joking joking joking so finally by the end of the night I'm like, I'm fucked up, she's hot, I'm a lesbian, I don't care if she's straight, I'm gonna make the move! So that's when I said, "You know, all this talk about getting married and we haven't even kissed." And the next thing I knew we're in the coat check humping each other.

–Angela, 27

At a Party

I was at a party and there was this girl there who had curly red hair and a porcelain face. She was wearing cut-off Victorian gloves and rhinestone bracelets and her fingers were all colored from painting or something and she had this kind of power thing that just caught me. It was her energy outside of being male or female that totally affected me. I have a very strong sexual presence so when somebody affects me like that they're usually very strong. So she walks up to me and says, "You're hot," and I say, "No, you're hot," and she says, "No, you're hot," and I say okay, and she gives me her number. It was very funny. And hot!

–Bridgette, 22

In Gay San Fran

I was 26 years old and visiting a friend from college in San Francisco. She showed me her giant box of sex toys and I got super turned on by it all. I'd never seen so many dildos, vibrators, dental dams, whips, handcuffs . . . I was breathless and just trying to be cool. We made jokes about how she'd always called me an honorary lesbo because I'm kind of butch and hung around with so many gay people. She'd always made cracks about how I should sleep with her at least once just so I could really earn my honorary title. I'd always make some smartass remark back at her and we'd punch each other in the arm and just party on. I never wanted to just because I wasn't into it. Well, there we were sitting on her bed and she was so beautiful. I was creamin' my jeans and she was cool—we both knew we were always just joking and I knew she wasn't going to come on to me. What I didn't know was that I was about to come on to her. We started kissing and giggling like little kids. She leaped out of bed and started grabbing things out of the toybox. We tried everything, some things twice.

—Michelle, 41

Anywhere, Anywhere at All, as Long as There's Booze:

> *All the times I've done it have involved drinking. Drinking puts me in the mood, and makes me not too terribly discerning how I . . . er . . . satisfy that mood. The first time was with this girl I met at a café where we were drinking. I was hanging out with the guy I was sleeping with at the time and she was at the table next to us. We started talking to her and she asked us if we were boyfriend and girlfriend. I told her we were just fuck buddies and she asked if she could be our fuck buddy too. We all went back to my place but when we got there the guy ended up being too drunk to hold up his end of the triangle, so it became me and the girl while he watched.*
>
> *–Marie, 25*

I couldn't help but notice that booze seemed to accompany a large percentage of first-time experiences. It seems a lot of women are really nervous and require a little social lubricant to nudge them forward. This is perfectly fine as long as you don't get shitfaced, because, as we all know, getting shitfaced usually involves making idiotic decisions and throwing caution to the wind. Likewise, if the girl you're hitting on is obliterated leave it alone; there are few people as disgusting as those who target the drunk as their sexual prey. But as far as calming the old nerves, a little libation can be just the thing. Here are some cocktails tailor-made for your girly endeavors.

bosom caresser

1 oz. Madeira
1 oz. brandy
½ oz. triple sec
Stir with ice and strain into a glass.

bushwhacker

½ oz. Amaretto
½ oz. coffee liqueur
½ oz. light rum
½ oz. Irish Cream liqueur
2 oz. light cream
Pour in a glass over ice.

fallen angel

Juice of 1 lime
1 ½ oz. gin
dash of bitters
½ tsp. crème de menthe
Shake with ice and strain into a glass. Serve with a cherry.

body shots

If you'd rather not waste time with all this shaking and mixing and stuff, nothing gets straight to the point like a body shot. For those of you who've never been on spring break, body shots are done as follows:

1. Find a hot chick.
2. Get two shots of tequila.
3. Find a sexy spot on her where her skin is exposed (collarbone, neck, cleavage, etc.)
4. Lick this spot and sprinkle some salt on it.
5. Stick a lime wedge in her mouth backward, with the rind inside her mouth and the meat of the fruit sticking out.
6. Down your shot of tequila, lick the salt off her body, and eat the lime out of her mouth.
7. Hand her her shot and have her do it to you.

Virtually Blind Dates

Another great way to meet women that I think deserves special mention is the personal ad. Long perceived of as a last-chance stop for desperate losers, this now incredibly popular way to make human contact can often be just the thing. Sure, there's something inherently depressing about looking for love in an ad, but let's face it, dating is the same thing as interviewing for a job. We're basically looking for qualified candidates with intelligence, skills, and creative ideas, who are team players and who look great bending over to pick up a pencil. Are you looking for a temp, part-time, or full-time position? Do you have experience? Are you going for a full-blown career change? Interview questions like "Where do you see yourself in five years?" in the dating world read as "What habits do you have that I think are so cute now but that will drive me nuts five years down the road?" So it makes sense to go about looking for a girl the same way you would go about finding a job. You're simply trying to find the right person, and there's no shame in that.

There are a plethora of online dating services, and nearly everything that calls itself a newspaper has a personal ads section. If you decide to try online, you can either do a search on "dating" or go to some of the sites I recommend in the back of the book. Most of them are free or practically free, and all of them have "Women Seeking Women" sections. Most of the online sites require you to set up a profile—fill out a questionnaire and post a picture of yourself. Then they put you in their online community, where you can browse through all their postings and respond to the ones you like as well as have other people see yours and contact you.

More traditional personal ads, like the ones that run in papers or that appear online at sites like Craig's List (www.craigslist.org), require you to write your own ad (as opposed to filling out a questionnaire). For these there's a system of shortcuts that you should be familiar with.

Personals Decoder

S=single, G=gay, L=lesbian, BI=bisexual, B=black, W=white, H=hispanic, A=asian, M=male, F=female, P=professional, N/S=non-smoker, N/D=no drugs, LTR=long term relationship, ISO=in search of, YO=years old

These abbreviations were developed in the days before the Internet, when everyone was running their ads in the paper and trying to save money by keeping them short, but a lot of them are still used even when space is unlimited.

If you do decide to place an ad, check out what other people have written to get some ideas. Depending on what you're looking for and how you want to come off, your ad can read a variety of different ways. Here are some suggestions.

Curious Straight Girl Looking for Same

31 YO, SW clitourist looking for like-minded traveling partner. Be discreet, and open, and don't freak out if I balk

at eating your pussy (I've never dined at the beaver bar before). Let's explore the unknown together.

Little Orphan Girl Looking for Daddy

Me: SBI submissive, in need of parental guidance.
You: big, fearless, lesbian, knows what to do with a Ping Pong paddle. Looking like John Candy a plus.

Help Me Please My Boyfriend

Hot, discreet couple ISO straight, bi, lesbian, whatever. Must be femme and into penetration. A knowledge of both foreign and domestic parts a plus but not required. Your picture gets ours.

Horny Beast Seeks Watering Hole

Straight, hot sexaholic seeks adventurous woman/women to ravage. I don't care what the hell you look like as long as you strap it on and can eat a mean pussy.

If you go the personals route, meet the person face to face as soon as possible. Someone can read great on the computer screen or in the paper, get you hot and bothered on the phone, and turn out to have ass breath and the sexual energy of a napkin in person. If there's no chemistry there's no deal, period. So don't waste your time and get your hopes up.

The most important thing to keep in mind is that all this is supposed to be fun. The stakes probably aren't as high as they are when you're looking for a boyfriend because you're probably less invested in it. This is an experiment. Like buying paper plates, not china. So don't psych yourself out. Take advantage of the fact that you get to be freer than ever; this will be great practice for just being yourself in a sexually charged situation. Who knows what will happen? Maybe you'll discover that you like it a lot more than you thought. Maybe you won't. At the very least, you'll learn something new. And it might even make you more sympathetic in the future to men who try to hit on you.

chapter four

Gettin' Some 101

Once you get over the fear that there's another woman in your bed and realize "I'm turned on, I want to fuck this chick," you'll know what to do. Having sex is a pretty organic thing.

—JOCELYN, 39

ow that we've been through the who, what, where, when, and why, it's time to get down and dirty with the how. If you're open enough and turned-on enough, you'll find that there's no end to the hot things you can do with another woman. Most of these things will just happen naturally when the situation presents itself (I mean, how much reading up have you done on the topic of fucking men?) but it never hurts to do a little research. Knowing some tricks of the trade can not only enable you to have more fun in bed but also might give you the extra confidence you need to get yourself there.

When discussing the logistics of sex between women, an interesting and unexpected question kept coming up: What *is* sex between women? In the hetero world, there seems to be a much clearer definition of sex: penile penetration. It's like unless he sticks his penis inside your vagina, it doesn't count. I always crack up when friends tell me they just fooled around with a guy but didn't actually fuck him, as if they were good little girls who would never go all the way until they knew him better. Meanwhile they're sucking his cock and rimming and titty-fucking and doing all sorts of other innocent things. Personally, I think it all counts. Why intercourse is rated above, say, oral sex is beyond me. You can take a nap while he's pumping away, you may never even see what his dick looks like, but if you're blowing him you're right there in the moment, you're getting to know his personals face to face.

The attachment to this "If it ain't penetration, it ain't fuckin'" dealio is not only silly but destructive. It automatically discredits girl-on-girl sex as sex unless there's a dildo involved, I guess, but even then it doesn't always count. I had a lesbian roommate who was quite the stud; I heard noises coming out of her bedroom that I didn't know women could make. During one of her sessions this genius I knew stopped by the house and was much impressed. He got all hot and bothered and wanted to know if he could get in on the action. I told him my roommate was a lesbian who wasn't interested in men—who'd never been with a man at all, actually. "So she's still a virgin?" He was appalled. I pointed out that virgins don't make women scream the way the woman in the next room was screaming. He wasn't having it, though. He just kept shaking his head and wondering how a 34-year-old woman could still be a virgin. I told him she wasn't. He insisted she was. I told him to leave.

This guy is an extreme case—although not an uncommon one, I fear—but in general there's quite a bit of confusion around the definition of girl-on-girl sex. Sex in the straight world even comes with the ever-popular baseball analogy: first base (kissing), second base (touching the boobies), third base (fingering), home run (intercourse). So how do you play ball with chicks?

Some women feel it doesn't count as sex unless you both have an orgasm. Some say sex is just an intimate connection with another person that's expressed both physically and emotionally. Some believe fingers, tongues, or toys have to be inserted, either anally or vaginally. Some say sex is a spiritual, not a physical, connection. Many straight girls feel they haven't "done it" unless they've gone down on another woman. "If you're mostly naked and your pussies are getting touched, that's sex," said Emily, 33.

What I concluded from all this is that if you feel like you've had sex, then you've had sex. No matter who you're fucking. If my friends feel that they haven't gone "all the way" with a guy until he sticks it in, that's their business. As far as I'm concerned, I've had sex with the vibrating seat beneath me on the subway.

I bring this up only because we're all stepping out of our normal routines here, and the definitions we've taken for granted for so long are getting challenged. The rules and the equipment are different and you may find yourself wondering for the first time, "Hmmmm, have I?" I'd hate for anyone to feel that since she hasn't tried some of the stuff I'm about to talk about, her experiences are suddenly void. There's no right or wrong way to have sex with a chick, and this is not a checklist. These are just some of the ways to get it on that I've come across in my travels. You can have just as sublime an experience with a couple of skilled fingers as you can with the most highfalutin strap-on, so don't worry if certain things don't appeal to you. This is sex, not a contest.

Before we get to the fun part, we need to spend a brief moment on the topic of safety. As most of you know, there's a plethora of nasty things you can catch from having unprotected sex: herpes, HPV, gonorrhea, chlamydia, syphilis, HIV . . . Some of these afflictions are curable, some aren't, and some are deadly, but luckily all can be avoided. How diligently you want to protect yourself is up to you; I get the feeling that when it comes to safe hetero-sexual sex, most women throw a condom on him before he sticks it in and then call it a day. Which does not fully pro-tect them, by any means, but it's all some people are will-ing to put up with. Because you're entering into a new situation with different body parts and different options, you're going to have to redefine what makes you feel safe enough to enjoy yourself. In order to do this properly, you need to be clear on what you're protecting yourself from and how it's possible to catch it.

What You Need to Know

The main thing you're protecting yourself from is the ex-change of bodily fluids, especially the passage of her blood into your bloodstream and vice versa. Blood-to-blood is the most direct and surefire way for you to get some of the most deadly diseases, like HIV, but there are plenty of other ways to catch that and many other things. HIV can also be passed through vaginal fluid and semen, and has been spotted in tears and saliva as well (although in lesser amounts). HIV can cause AIDS, which can cause you to die.

Genital herpes is spread when the gunk from a herpes sore comes into contact with the bloodstream (via a cut or open sore) or with the mucous membranes found in the mouth, vagina, penis, and anus—meaning you can get it from such things as giving oral sex, from humping pussies, and from touching hers and then touching yours. Although herpes isn't contagious when it's not active, the blisters can sometimes be hard to see, and it's also possible to transmit the virus immediately before and after outbreaks. One of the many, many sucky things about herpes is that it's incurable. It's also highly contagious, and outbreaks can be violently painful. There are drugs you can take every day for the rest of your life to prevent outbreaks from happening, but better to avoid herpes in the first place.

Let's see, then there's HPV (human papillomavirus), which causes anogenital warts. It's spread a lot like herpes, is also incurable, and sometimes also causes cervical cancer. Then there are the hepatitises A, B, and C. A can be gotten from eating feces, meaning fans of rimming (the licking of buttholes) are at high risk. Hepatitis A isn't very dangerous and can be treated. Hepatitis B is transmitted through blood, vaginal fluids, and semen. It can screw up your liver if it gets out of hand, but there's a vaccine for it and it's also treatable. Hepatitis C is the real motherfucker of the three, as it's incurable and can terminally damage your liver. It's only transmittable through blood.

Chlamydia, gonorrhea, and syphilis are bacterial and are passed through sexual contact involving the mouth, genitals, and anus. They can be really uncomfortable but are treatable with antibiotics. Trichomoniasis is a parasitic infection that's passed through sexual contact and sharing sex toys. It's uncomfortable but not terribly dangerous if treated right away. Crabs are vile little lice that hang out in your pubic hair and are transmitted by bumping uglies and/or crawling into bed or sharing clothes with an infested person. They can be gotten rid of but they itch like hell and make you feel like you have bugs crawling on you. Which you do.

What You Need to Use

As daunting and disgusting as this all may sound, there is hope and plenty of fun still to be had. Luckily, there's an endless supply of artillery, latex and otherwise, to combat all these obnoxious STDs. It may not be as much fun as ripping off your clothes and ho-ing down with reckless abandon, but safe sex is just one of those things, like wearing a motorcycle helmet or checking your caller ID, that averts disaster by infringing on your spontaneity just a tiny little bit. I'm going to list a bunch of ways to protect yourself and you can decide which ones work best for you.

Condoms

Even though there's no penis involved, condoms are a vital part of girl-on-girl sex. They're hugely important if you're using dildos, vibrators, cucumbers, or anything else to stick inside yourself and your lover. If you use a dildo on yourself, first cover it with a condom. Anything you stick inside yourself should be cleaned thoroughly or re-condomed before it goes in her, because sharing un-condomed sex toys without washing them is an excellent way to pass on cooties. Using a condom makes life a lot easier, because you don't have to get up out of bed and scrub down your toys in the middle of a hot moment. All you have to do is take a second to change condoms, and you're on your way. Likewise, if you stick anything up your butt (or hers) it should have a condom on it that you change before it goes up your vagina (or hers). In a pinch, a condom can also be cut down the side and used as a dental dam (make sure it's nonlubed, or it'll taste nasty) or slipped on your finger and used as a cot (finger condoms).

There are so many different kinds of condoms to choose from it's hard to know what the fuck. Basically, they're made out of latex, lambskin, or polyurethane and are either lubed or nonlubed. Latex condoms are the most durable, the cheapest, and the easiest to find. They come in a huge variety of shapes, colors, and sizes and are pretty much your safest bet, because they do a good job of blocking the microbes that cause STDs. The downside is that they can deteriorate in intense heat, so if you're having a marathon session you should change your condom somewhere along the way. Many people are allergic to latex, which makes polyurethane their best option. Polyurethane condoms aren't as elastic as latex but they, too, prevent the passage of sexually transmitted diseases. They're a bit harder to find and more expensive but a must-have if you're allergic to latex. Lambskin condoms are useless for our needs. They feel great on men, but are useful only in preventing pregnancy and don't do squat to prevent the passing of STDs.

Lubed or nonlubed, that is the question. Since we're mostly concerned here with how condoms can be best used with sex toys, nonlubed is the way to go. Not only will nonlubed condoms allow you to use the lube of your choice (which you'll absolutely need to do) but the silicone in some condom lubes can damage your silicone sex toys. Check out the lube section later in this chapter to figure out which lube is for you.

Dental Dams

I don't know why these are even sold in sex stores any-more—there are much better and safer options out there—but they are. Dental dams are little latex squares used by dentists to isolate a tooth or something (I'm not sure exactly how that works, but I don't believe we care). When the need for safe sex reared its ugly head, people who wanted to partake in cunnilingus and rimming scooped them up to use as barriers. At the time it made perfect sense—dams are thin and elastic, and they come in a variety of colors and flavors; all you have to do is spread the sheet over the desired area and go at it, making sure to hold the dam in place and keep her bits covered at all times. Yet because they were originally designed for use by dentists, they aren't ideal for oral sex. They're too small and can be hard to hold on to. They're also a little thicker and clunkier than the Glyde dam, which I recommend because it was specifically designed for oral sex. I'd pretty much only use a dental dam if I was trapped on a deserted island with nothing but a hot chick and a dentist's office.

Glyde Dams

These much bigger, thinner, and silkier rectangular latex rectangles are the Cadillacs of latex dams. Designed specifically for eating ass and pussy, Glyde dams provide a silky, sexy layer between you and your partner that's big enough to do the job (roughly 10 x 6 inches). They also come in various colors and flavors and are much safer than dental dams because they give you more to grip on to. If you use lube, which I recommend, be sure to use a water-based one and put a dab on her vagina or anus for more slippery fun. Then just place the barrier on her crotch and your mouth on the barrier, and munch away. When using a dam, remember which side was used for which: you can drop the dam if you come up for air or switch positions, and putting your mouth on the side that was just on her pussy defeats the whole purpose. If you can't find Glyde dams at a sex store near you, go to sheerglydedams.com.

Plastic Wrap

The plastic wrap once used by mothers everywhere to cover casseroles and pack up batches of wholesome brownies has now been taken over by sex fiends, making housewives everywhere suddenly suspect ("Hmmm, Mrs. Jimmerson certainly goes through a lot of Saran Wrap"). Plastic wrap makes an excellent barrier for cunnilingus, humping, and anal munching. You can rip it off in sheets as big as you want and you can even make her a pair of panties out of it. It's also great because it's cheaper than buying dams and it's not latex so if you're allergic it's a-okay. Above all, there's usually some lying around the house.

Gloves

There are many reasons to wear gloves when getting it on with the ladies. Gloves will protect you if you have any cuts on your fingers or hands. They'll protect both of you from sharing goodies from vagina to vagina or anus to vagina. If you're fingering her butthole and decide you'd like to now strap it on while you finger your own pussy, for instance, all you need to do is remove the glove and either put on another or fly free. You can appoint your ungloved hand for a specific area, using a glove for all others if you want, but then you must pay attention. If you're fingering her asshole, a nice lubed latex finger might feel better than a rough hand with a fingernail on top.

Be sure to use nonlatex gloves if either of you is allergic (you can find these in some medical supply stores), and always take off your rings so they don't break the glove. If you've got long-ass porn-star fingernails and refuse to cut them, perhaps wearing a glove will save her innards from being impaled. Gloves can also double as barriers—cut one up the side and spread it over her pussy (make sure it's a powder-free glove, or it'll taste nasty). You can use the fingers of the glove to send your tongue in deep or as a shield for sliding your own fingers in and out.

Finger Cots

These individual little latex tubes go over your finger, like a finger condom. They're fabulous because they protect you both and aren't quite as involved as a glove. You can find them in pharmacies and sex stores. As with all things latex, be sure to use lube with them before sliding them into any holes.

Lube Aroonie

We women have the natural ability to create our own lube, but sometimes we might need to ask for a little outside help. If sex goes on for hours on end or if it happens underwater or if you're using sex toys or nonlubed condoms, for example, only those with lube glands the size of fire hoses won't need assistance. The rest of us will need some store-bought reinforcements to keep things juicy. And keeping things juicy is of the utmost importance. Not only does lube make everything feel slippery and sexy, but it prevents vaginas, buttholes, and condoms from getting rubbed raw, ripped, or torn. Lube is also essential with sex toys, as it is anytime you stick anything up your ass since your poor anus has no way to make lube of its own. Basically, if you're having sex, lube should be there.

There are so many different kinds of lube on the market today it's hard to know which is the one for you, but you can narrow it down depending on what you need. If you're using silicone sex toys, stay away from silicone-based lubes, which can damage your toys. Oil-based lubes (like baby oil, Vaseline, and lotion) can be fun to rub on nipples and use for massages, but they can wreak havoc on the vagina and should never be used for sex. Oil is not only really hard for the vagina to get rid of but it can change your pH balance, leading to all sorts of not-fun bacterial growth and infections. Then there's good old K-Y jelly, which has hardly any staying power since it was invented for medical use, not rowdy sex. It's pretty much obsolete in the sex world nowadays since there are so many better slippery options—including K-Y Liquid, which the manufacturer created with sex, not prostate exams, in mind. Water-based lubes are the most common and are available in the widest variety. Big crowd pleasers are the kinds that contain glycerin. These lubes are usually thin and slick, and when they start to dry out and get sticky, all you have to do is add a little water or saliva rather than more lube, and you're up and running again. How great is that?

Base your decision on how slippery the lube is, how sticky it gets, how long it lasts, its thickness, taste, price, and ingredients, and your body's reactions. Many sex stores nowadays sell sample packets of lube so you can take a whole bunch of different kinds home and test them out. Check the chart below to see which ones will work best for you.

WHICH LUBE IS YOUR LUBE?

	PROS	CONS
WATER-BASED WITH GLYCERIN	Super-easy to clean up Comes in a variety of flavors Latex compatible Thin, slippery texture Can be reactivated with water or saliva Stays slippery longer than nonglycerin water-based	Glycerin causes yeast infections in some women Doesn't last as long as silicone-based lubes
WATER-BASED WITHOUT GLYCERIN	Super-easy to clean up Thin, slippery texture Latex compatible	Dries out faster than glycerin lubes Have to reapply often, (the water/saliva trick won't work here)
ALL-NATURAL WATER-BASED	Made with all-natural ingredients to keep horny hippies happy Super-easy to clean up Latex compatible Thin, slippery texture	Not as slippery as most lubes Need to reapply often Harder to find

	PROS	CONS
SILICONE-BASED	Unstoppably slick Water-resistant Never, ever dries up Latex compatible Doesn't contain glycerin Best anal sex lube there is	Really hard to clean up Not usable with silicone toys Hard for vagina to flush out
OIL-BASED	Super-slippery Easy to find	Not compatible with latex Impossible for vagina to flush out Causes pH imbalances in some women

WARNING: Don't use any lube with Nonoxynol-9 in it. Nonoxynol-9 is a chemical that was originally put in lubricants because it kills sperm, HIV, and other sexually transmitted diseases—but then they discovered it can also cause teeny-tiny tears in your vaginal and anal walls, making it easier for these diseases to get into your bloodstream. It also causes major burning and itching and weird allergic reactions in many people. But they still put it in lubes and it's found in a lot of lubricated condoms. Hello? So read your labels, people.

Let's Get It On!

Okay, now that we've got that out of the way, we can get down to the good stuff. Up until this point it's been all about sex with another woman as it exists in your head. It's been about picking sex apart and fantasizing about it, but now it's about facing it head-on with a real live woman. It would suck to get this far and suddenly have fear hog-tie you, yet it's here, right before you take the plunge, that you're most likely to decide that this was a stupid idea and what the hell are you doing here anyway, cuz you're straight for fuck's sake! This is where the kiss comes in. If you can just shut your mind up long enough to plant a kiss on her, this mighty little gesture will pick up your insurmountable anxieties and hurl them out the window.

> The main difference between being with a woman and a man is it felt so charged and naughty. It was never this slow, easy build-up with women. It's like once you start kissing you just can't stop.
>
> —PAM, 33

You will have successfully crossed over into the physical realm and, as any good ho-bag knows, once it gets physical it gets hard to stop. Kissing is a gateway drug to sex.

The kiss takes matters from the hypothetical to the real and, assuming she's a decent kisser, it can get all sorts of juices flowing, juices that will drown out any second thoughts that might come along and try to mess up your good time.

> The kissing is different, it's so much softer and sensual. Even how their bodies feel, they're softer and warmer.

—LINDA, 41

Now that the game is on, you get to discover where all her hot spots are. You pretty much can't swing a dead cat at a woman's body without hitting an erogenous zone, but what feels good can be different for each person. You know from your own body where you like to be touched, so that's a good place to start; then just feel your way around and notice her reactions. Some people like to be touched softly, others like it rough, and some like both. I recommend starting off softly; if you feel like increasing the intensity, do it slowly and pay close attention—if she moans when you squeeze her nipples, do it harder and harder until she grabs your hand. The following is a list of things to do and places to go.

Scalp: The scalp is full of nerves and loves to be massaged and scratched. Gather a bunch of hair in your fist close to the scalp and slowly pull.

Face: Run your hand, lips, and tongue along her cheekbones, lips, eyes, and forehead. Lick her lips and kiss her eyes.

Ears: Outline the back, top, and inside with your fingers. Tug and massage her earlobes. Run your tongue up her neck and inside her ear.

Neck: Tickle, kiss, nibble, and lick her nape. Light teasing pecks will work as well as digging your face in there.

I had a massive orgasm once from having someone do nothing but make out with the back of my neck.

—CHRIS, 29

Tits: If you play around with tits they release a hormone called oxytocin which causes tingling sensations in the genitals. Stroke, tickle, and kiss them. Get behind her and really get a handful. Massage baby oil onto them. Take her nipple in your mouth and suck on it, pinch it between your lips, and bite it, harder and harder, until she can't take it anymore.

I love to have a chick rest her tits on my eyes and let the natural weight of the breasts press down on me. Like those bean bags you put on your eyes but better because they're tits!

—AMY, 34

Belly: Lick, tickle, and kiss. Draw little designs with your finger or tongue. Since her belly is so close to her crotch, toying with this area can make her go crazy with anticipation.

Buttocks: Butt cheeks are loaded with nerve endings. Some people are super-ticklish here, but for those who aren't, massaging, kneading, kissing, licking, and spanking can feel mighty fine.

Fingers and Toes: These'll be less hairy and softer than the ones you're used to. Suck, nibble, tug, and massage them.

Once you learn where she wants you to go, then you get to discover what she wants you to do. There's an infinite number of ways for women to get it on. There are endless positions, combinations of moves, uses for toys, ways to kiss, lick, stroke, spank, finger, rub, pinch . . . you could fuck for thirty days straight and still not get to everything. Right now I'm going to cover some of the fun things you can do when it's just you and her and a bottle of lube. I've decided to save cunnilingus for its own chapter, because this is a book for straight girls and, while it is true that some chicks can't get their faces in there fast enough, nothing scares the shit out of scared straight girls more than eating pussy. They act as though women have this soft and sexy candy-coated outside, and a cave full of seaweed between their legs. This topic clearly needs special attention, so I think we'll take it slow, get down with the basics first, and save sniffing the pretty pansy for later.

Fingering

Being in the hands of someone who really knows how to use a finger is one of my favorite places to be, whether that finger's attached to a male or a female. Fingers are the most versatile sex toys on the earth. You can control how they move, how hard or soft they press and pinch, and how quickly they rub. You can use one, three, or all ten, and in different combinations. When someone hits just the right spot with just the right pressure at just the right time it's incredible, like they're reading my mind—which really is sort of what you have to do to be any good at it. You have to think about all the hot spots and imagine you can feel what you're doing to them. Like when you're giving a guy a hand job—you have to imagine what he's feeling and what would feel good to him. Luckily, with women you have a better sense of what works. Pay attention while fingering yourself and her. Elaborate on some of the moves your lovers have tried on you. Masturbate side by side with your lover and notice how she fingers herself. Maybe even spend an entire evening without any oral sex or any toys— just have a full-on fingerfest and see what you come up with. Chances are very good you won't be disappointed. Here are some techniques to store away in your finger file:

Techniques

1. *The Petting Zoo.* Lay her down on her back and gently run your fingers through her pubic hair. Tug on it gently; then press down on her mound, using your whole palm to rub her entire mound and clit.
2. *The Double-Handed Screwball.* Cross your middle finger over your index finger and slide them in and out of her vagina like a screw. Do this while you put a dab of lube on her clit and rub it in quick circles with your other hand. Keep fucking her with the fingers of one hand while you rub her clit with your other.

3. *Whassup G?* Stick two fingers inside her and bend them forward (toward her belly button). Locate her G-spot and rub it while you press the palm of the same hand down on her clit and "grab" her pubic bone. Slide your entire hand up and down while you rub your fingers on her G-spot.

4. *The Big Tease.* Run your middle finger back and forth from her vagina to her clit, dipping inside her to get some lube. Start by gently teasing her with one finger before adding more to the mix and pressing down harder.

5. *Playing with Marbles.* Take her glans between your finger and thumb and gently squeeze and roll it around—pay close attention to her reaction, as the clit is supersensitive (it's a good idea to include some skin from the hood to cut down on the sensitivity). Lightly tap tap tap her clit with your fingers while you use your thumb on her vagina.

6. *Wax On, Wax Off.* Put a dab of lube on the pads of your middle and forefinger and slowly rub them around in big wide luscious circles on her clit. Vary how much you press down, starting lightly and increasing the pressure as you go. Change the direction of your circles for a while, increasing the speed. Start using the tips of your fingers, and wiggle them

around while you continue circling, as if they're walking on her clit.

7. *Chopstick Lips.* Lay your hand flat on her vulva and scissor the lips of her inner labia, using the entire length of your middle and forefinger. Squeeze and tug on her lips; press down and rub (remember that the clit runs all the way underneath her labia, so it feels really good). While you tug on her lips, use the tips of your fingers to massage her glans.

vocabulary builder

PUDDLE JUMPING:
switching back and forth from fingering her to fingering yourself

Depending on how your bodies are positioned, some of these techniques will be easier than others. In general, getting into position for fingering is a breeze compared to some other activities like going pussy to pussy or 69ing, because you have a lot more options—you have an entire arm span to work with, so you can be much more creative and access each other from many different vantage points. Here's a list of good positions to try out:

🍒 Lie side by side facing each other. Slowly trace her body with your finger, starting from her face and going all the way down to her pussy. Use one hand to squeeze her tits, pull her hair, or spank her butt while you finger her with the other. This position is nice because it gives you as much access to her whole body as it gives her to yours.

SITTING V

🍒 Have her sit with her legs together while you straddle her, your legs stretched out in a V shape resting on top of hers. Grind your pussys together while you slide your hand between your bodies and get a fingerful.

- Both of you sit up and face each other cross-legged. This position gives you nice wide-open access to her pussy, and vice versa–it's great for G-spot stimulation as well.

- Lie on top of her, pussy to pussy, and finger her from the top (meaning your hand is sliding down the crack of your own ass to reach her pussy). Try fingering her and yourself at the same time, using the fingers for her and your thumb for yourself.

- Bend her over onto all fours and kneel behind her, pressing your pussy up against her ass. Reach underneath and finger her pussy while you rub yours up against her ass. While you're at it, reach around and grab her tits or pull her hair.

- Have her lie or sit with her crotch at the edge of the bed while you sit on the floor facing her. Because you have such easy access, this is a great position to work on her pussy with two hands.

- Sit on the edge of the bed and have her lie across your lap with her crotch right by your knees for easy access. Spread her legs and finger her from above. Feel free to pull her hair while you're at it.

LAPTOP FINGERING

🍒 Lay her on her back and get on all fours on top of her, with your face facing her pussy in a 69ish position. Stay on all fours, sit up, or slump over, giving her pussy a nice rub down with your titties if you please.

Sandy, 38, offers up this one:

I love this position because it's like fucking and masturbating at the same time. Sit your partner up and slide behind her so your chest is pressing against her back. Spread her legs and then spread yours behind hers, pushing her ass against your pussy. Reach around in front of her and stroke her pussy. Use your other hand to grab her tits or her hair. Slide your fingers inside her while you rub her clit with your thumb. This is a great position because you can really get in there with your fingers and fuck her hard while you grind her ass into your pussy. You can finger fuck her or spread her legs wide and rub circles on her clit or both. This is a fun one if you're having a three-way where someone else is watching because they can really see what you're doing.

WRAPAROUND

A good variation on the one above is to have her lie on top of you, her back to your front, while you reach up and finger her from below.

> I think when a lot of men finger a woman it's more to get her going, it's like a route to getting their dicks in there. With another chick it can be the main event, which means it takes more time and is done with much more creativity.
>
> —ROXANNE, 37

Humping

I must admit, before I tried this with another woman I was really skeptical. I expected it to be okay, but to lack so much compared to doing it with a guy. With a guy you get all that grinding *plus* penile penetration! Girl-on-girl humping seemed ho-hum, like the sort of thing you do when you're half asleep in the middle of the night and too lazy to move. But I was wrong, oh so wrong! Bumping doughnuts with another chick is awesome. I think the fact that you both have clits and are both as into the grinding process makes this incredibly pleasurable. I've been with guys who totally focus on hitting the right spot for me, but with another chick she's hitting it for you *and* for her, which is totally exciting in a different way. Plus you can rub your tits against hers while you're doing it. Hot again. *Plus* it's such an easy thing to whip out anywhere—you don't even have to take off your clothes, so you can do it on the damn dance floor if you feel like it. Here are some great ways to do it.

Lying Down

🍒 The meat-and-potatoes version of missionary face-to-face is always a goodie. Start off by softly sliding your mound and outer lips onto hers (this feels especially fabulous if you've both been waxed or shaved and if you stick a little lube down there). Soak up the feeling of pussy on pussy before you get into the grind. Then lie down on her fully and use your body weight to put pressure on both your clits. If you need more, put one arm behind her back and one behind her ass and pull her as closely into you as you can. Kiss her, tease her, roll around and change who's on top and who's on the bottom.

🍒 Lay her on her back and push her legs together. Climb on top and straddle her, either holding yourself up with your arms or lying down on top of her. Try holding her wrists down to the bed, and fucking her hard. Put one leg in between hers and go at an angle. Rub baby oil on your chests and rub your whole bodies together. Mix it up by playing with her pussy: stick your fingers in her and rub her G-spot while you grind her clit with yours. Stick your thumb up your own pussy and fuck her with your fingers at the same time while you grind.

- While she's lying on her back, lie down next to her on your side and hump her thigh, using your own thigh to grind into her pussy.

- Lie on top of her backward, with your feet by her head, with her facing up and you facing down. Scissor your legs together by sliding one leg under her while keeping the other on top, moving toward each other until your pussies are pressed right up against each other. Move around in this position until you hit a spot that feels good for you both and grind away.

Sitting, Etc.

- Have her sit in a chair while you straddle her and sit on top of her. Use the back of the chair to pull yourself into her, and use your legs to position your pussy just right. Grind yourself into her while she sucks on your tits.

SCISSORS

Both of you lie on your backs and hold yourselves up in a semisitting position with your arms. Face each other and slide your legs together into a scissor position, moving closer and closer until your pussies press together. You can remain holding yourselves up with your arms or come to a full sitting position and hug, pulling each other closer together and grinding hard.

The scissors is one of my favorite positions because it's like your pussies are making out. It's like a sex seal, you can move around and dictate what you're going to feel. It feels fucking good!

—AMY, 34

Standing

🍒 Stand up and pin her against the wall. Grind the front of your pussy into the front of hers. Hold her wrists and make out, or pull her hair and grab her ass. For variation, spread her legs slightly and slide your thigh in between, grinding her pussy with your leg while you hump her thigh.

🍒 Have her sit on a countertop or table that's the same height as your crotch. Pull her pussy all the way to the edge while you, standing, press yours into hers.

Anal Sex

Another treat I highly recommend is getting some sweet girl to stick something up your ass, especially if you've never gone there before. The nice thing about trying anal for the first time with a chick is you can take your time. You don't have to worry about her losing her hard-on, which means slow and steady can win the race. And that really can make or break the deal, as some women really need a lot of time to take it all in. Anal penetration can be painful, but if you relax, communicate with your partner, and use a shitload of lube, you can get it in there and really have a good time. Trust me, the pain gives way to some of the most intense pleasure I've ever felt. I love it up the butt, Bob, and I hope you will, too.

Before you get into anal play with toys (which I'll discuss in Chapter 6, "Pandora's Toybox,") it's best to get familiar with it using just fingers. Stick on a glove and put plenty of lube on your finger. Gently rub her butthole, teasing it and pressing down on it. Slowly enter her, moving your finger in slow circles as you go. Pump your finger in and out of her ass while you caress her clit with your other hand. Press on her anal canal; stroke her inside while you pull your finger in and out. Put on more lube and slowly put another finger up her (make sure to keep an eye on her response—if she's not relaxed enough, this might be a little painful). Pump your fingers in and out while you rub her clit with your thumb. Once she relaxes and just goes with the feeling, she can really begin to enjoy this and you can begin to add more fingers.

I think there's a lot of unnecessary fear around anal sex—people whine about how it hurts, that it's messy, that it'll stretch your butthole out for good. It can hurt if you ram something up there without warming up first, and it can be a little messy or not messy at all. And as for stretching you out, you have two sphincters and they are both tight and resilient little soldiers. They will not stretch out unless you stick a bowling ball up there, and even then you might be able to bounce back.

There's obviously a buttload of other things you can do together (many of which you'll read about in the next few chapters), but this should get you started. While you're diving in, keep in mind that sex with another woman is still sex. I think because it's not with the gender we're used to having it with, some women act like it's some big mysterious thing. But in reality, a lot of the same rules apply.

> I think society makes women with women seem more kinky than it is. It's really just normal and great but everyone who's not doing it wants it to be this crazy freaky thing.
>
> —SUSAN, 20

If you're not comfortable with the other person, chances are it won't be such a great experience. If she doesn't make you feel hot, and if you don't think she's hot, same deal. Some physical and/or psychological connection is usually needed for sex to be any good (depending on how wasted you are). So don't think you can just jump in the sack with any old chick and have it be awesome just because you can't wait to try it. But if you set yourself up properly and hook up with someone you're hot for, chances are excellent you'll have a great time. Just let yourself go and have fun with it.

chapter five

Oh My God, She Wants Me to Eat Her Pussy!

It was soft and smooth and had a bit of a metallic taste. I was pleasantly surprised.

—DONNA, 29

Here's the thing. If you sit down and really think about sex in the most basic way, there are plenty of things about it that sound less than appealing. Take blow jobs, for example. An erect penis enters your mouth, sometimes after a long day of much pissing and hanging around with sweaty balls. As it goes deep into your throat, possibly eliciting a little gag action, your nose is pressed against a pair of hairy balls or maybe even a butthole. You suck it in and out and in and out, usually losing some drool on his thigh, and then the whole experience is topped off with a mouthful of semen.

Me, I love giving blow jobs; it's one of my all-time favorite things to do. And when I try to think way back to before I ever did it, I don't remember being that freaked out about it. I do remember gagging once or twice when I got down to it, but it never stopped me in my tracks the way eating pussy seems to stop a lot of dick-lovin' straight girls. I mean, how much worse could eating pussy be? How come everything's all hunky-dory, kissing, petting, having her go down on you, but when it comes time to dine at the beaver bar, many women get squirrely and don't want to play anymore?

I have a couple of theories. One is that we're thinking about it waaaay too much. Because we're mostly driven in a heterosexual direction, and that direction is far more socially acceptable and hence much less scrutinized, having sex with men is just something we do naturally, without giving it a ton of thought. But sleeping with women is taboo and new and a little scary, so we pick it apart. If it exists as a thought in your head long before you actually do it, you have plenty of time to analyze the reality, which isn't very sexy at all. Really getting down and thinking about sex is like really getting down and thinking about eating meat—it can turn something wonderfully decadent into something that makes you gag.

Another problem is that we're buying into this image of the cunt as an oozy, yeasty, stinky fish farm. I don't know about you, but I'm not being followed around by a swarm of flies. Our capacity to believe our pussies are nasty is up there with believing we're too fat or too stupid. Stick your finger down there right now and take a little taste. Smell it and see if it makes you run for the toilet. Nearly everyone I talked to was pleasantly surprised at how untraumatic going down on a chick was. I mostly got comments like "Not gross. Salty," "It tasted like me!" "It hardly smelled at all, maybe a little sweaty and sexy." This is not to say that muff diving was loved by all, but very few women were actually turned off by it. Plus, if it was really scary and less than fresh, do you think men would be lining up to do it? I don't think so.

Straight girls also suffer from a lot of performance anxiety. It's like there's a team of judges who wave you by on stuff like fingering, kissing, and boob play, but when it gets to eating pussy they all lean up in their chairs and grip their scorecards. It's like someone told you this is the true measure of just how big a bisexual stud you are. Of course you're not going to know exactly what you're doing if you've never done it before, but you have instincts and you can read her reactions. Plus, you've had someone do it to you—I hope!—so you can try out the stuff you like on her. If you spend the whole time worrying instead of getting into it and really feeling it, you'll most definitely suck at it. So stop acting like her pussy is glaring at you screaming "Eat me, straight girl!" and just enjoy it, fer fuck's sake.

Another possibility is that eating pussy raises the same fears in women as getting it up the ass does in men. If we like it, are we homos? Because both these experiences are Big Nasty Scaries, liking them is perceived as pushing the envelope over the straight edge into certain gaydom. Which is a tad overdramatic. Being gay or straight has just as much to do with what's between your ears as it does with what's between your legs, so unless it rocks your world psychologically as well as physically, you're probably just plain old pussy-lovin' horny girl. And if it turns out you *are* really into it, lucky you for finding out who you really are and what it is that really makes you happy.

Oh My God, She Has Her Period!

Before we go any deeper into the pussy, I feel we must first pause for a menstrual moment. When discussing the topic of eating pussy, our little red friend came up over and over again as the dreaded enemy. As Miranda, thirty, so eloquently put it: "I've seen what comes out of mine; I sure as hell don't want to eat what comes out of hers"—which leads me to believe that some women are not only scared of other women's periods, they're scared of their own.

Before you can even start to try and wrap your head around the idea of dealing with hers, you have to embrace yours. As someone who suffers from incapacitating cramps and a nearly uncontainable blood flow, I'm not saying you should be jumping for joy when it's your time of the month, but you shouldn't be grossed out or pissed off by it, either. It's your body doing its thing. There's something cool about it, like it's a special secret that only women understand that bonds us all together and gives us the staggering privilege of growing new life. I'm always amazed that my body knows what it's doing, that its clock works so well and that it knows how to flush itself out. That's as hippie-dippie as I'm going to get about it, but I really urge you to rethink this if you have a negative attitude. What if you never got your period again? Wouldn't you feel a little bit of a loss, like you no longer had to check in with your femininity once a month? Try changing your perspective and how you talk about it and I guarantee that it'll become a much more pleasurable experience.

When it comes to dealing with hers, keep in mind how you'd like to be treated. Think about how awful it would feel if someone treated you like a slimy beast for having the audacity to bleed when she wanted to dine out. Even the most subtle hint of being grossed out can make someone feel pretty disgusting. If going down on a girl while she's bleeding is not for you, just do other things instead. The more unfazed you are about it, the more comfortable she'll feel. And if she's not into going down on you while you're bleeding, don't make a big deal about it. Nobody should have to do anything she doesn't want to. But if you do decide you want to give it a try, here are a couple of options:

Use a barrier. Stick some plastic wrap or a latex dam between you and her pussy. This will keep the blood at bay and will also protect you. Some of the scariest things are passed from person to person through blood, so you need to be extra careful.

Use a tampon. This is a great way to keep the blood out of your party. It doesn't give you much access to her vagina, but as there are many other parts to play with, a tampon is an excellent option.

Now that we've got some concerns under control, I'll offer up some helpful cunt-lickin' tips, gathered from experts the world over. I hope these will up both your technique and your confidence.

Pussy tastes and smells like a dead fish.

Southern Hospitality

There are many specifics to being a good eater-outer as well as some general rules that you should keep in mind. First, it's not all about the clit. She's definitely the queen of the prom, but the official boundaries of cunnilingus range from the top of the pubic mound to the back of the perineum. (If your mouth hits her asshole, you're out of bounds—you've officially crossed the line into rimming.) Let your mouth roam over this entire incredibly sensitive area and discover which spots do it for her. Second, it's not all about your mouth. Things like fingers, toys, water, and your chin can all be brought in to add to the experience. Experiment with different combinations and methods. Also, take your time. You know how much better it is when you're with a guy and he warms you up instead of just sticking it in and banging away. Same goes for eating pussy. Work up to the part where you're really cramming your head in there and sucking on her clit. Wake up all her nerve endings and let her feel the sensation of each lick first.

It's also nice to tease your way down her body before your mouth gets to her crotch. Let her know it's coming, but take your time getting there. Rhythm is key, as well. Don't spend too long doing the same thing over and over, or she'll get bored. And don't switch from licking to biting to sucking too fast, or she'll never get into it. If you start doing something and she responds by grabbing your hair or clenching her thighs, keep going! Change what you're doing slowly, and pause on whatever she responds to. And, last but not least, keep in mind that every woman is different. Just because you go through the roof when someone nibbles on your clit doesn't mean someone else couldn't find this painful or annoying. Pay attention to her reactions and proceed from there.

> The first time I wasn't nervous at all. I was really centered on eating her out because I didn't know if I'd ever be in this position again and that's the thing I was most curious about.
>
> —ALEXIS, 33

When going down on your girl, you might want to start out in this classic muff-munching position: have her lie on her back on the bed with her knees bent towards the ceiling and her legs slightly spread. Kneel down in front of her pussy with your legs folded beneath you and your torso bent forward, using your arms to prop you up if you need extra support. If you'd like a better angle and easier access to her pussy, try sliding some pillows beneath her butt.

Once you're there, eye to eye with the happy hamster, keep in mind that you have a plethora of helpful tools at your disposal to get the job done with flying colors. Yet, as with all tools, unless you know what they are and how to use them they're useless. The following section will help you be all you can be:

Your God-Given Tool Box

The Tongue

The cool thing about your tongue is that, relative to its size, it's the strongest muscle in your body. At the same time it's also soft and sensual. The tongue is, without a doubt, the most valuable tool when eating out a woman, so take advantage of its versatility and get creative with it. It's a pleasure tool for both you and her, providing her with a variety of sensations while letting you feel and taste everything that's going on. There are a bunch of highly touted ways to use this impressive little muscle.

🍒 Switch back and forth from pointy to flat. Begin your exploration by outlining the whole area with a nice pointed tongue. Lightly run it along her perineum and up both sides of her vagina to the hood. Use it lightly, like a tickler, giving her just the bare minimum of sensation. Tease her for a while and then flatten it out and lick her mound; open your mouth wide and run it all the way up. Keep it relaxed and soft and gently lick her entire labia with a flat, wide tongue, as if you were licking an ice cream cone. Go slowly from bottom to top and from side to side, increasing the pressure of your tongue with each lick.

Pretend like you're eating an ice cream cone, the best ice cream you've ever had. It's a huge ice cream cone and you want to get every little bit and you're just loving it. Lick and slurp and bite and get every last drop. For some reason this works really well. In fact, after I tried this on a woman, I told my boyfriend to try it because he wasn't actually great at eating pussy, and I swear it improved his performance.
–Jeannie, 32

As her excitement builds, you can start to add more pressure. Focus on the area around the clit and start making shorter, more concentrated licks, like a cat lapping milk. Take her hood in your mouth and suck on it while flicking her clit with a sharp, pointed tongue. Release it and continue to flick her clit, increasing the speed as you go. (If you're hitting her right on her glans, not through her hood, make sure she's okay, because this can be intense.) Move your tongue in circles around her clit; flatten your tongue out and increase the pressure, really pressing it in there and continuing with the circles.

- A fluttering, active tongue is one of the most widely appreciated tricks of cunnilingus. Keeping it moving all over, from labia to clit, can be incredibly pleasurable. A popular method is spelling out the alphabet. I've heard this tip from several people, and have had it done to me and I love it. The alphabet sends the tongue to all corners of your pussy in all sorts of different patterns. Try it with a flat tongue as well as a pointed one. Use varying amounts of pressure and different-sized letters.

- Tonguing her vagina is also yummy. Point your tongue and outline her hole, dipping in and licking it on all sides. Stick your tongue all the way in and grip her pubic bone with your whole mouth. Flick your tongue in and out with quick, intense movements and massage her inner walls with firm rotations.

When it came to going down on her, it was surreal and didn't seem like it could be me. Then THERE IT WAS. HER CLIT. UNDER MY TONGUE. I COULD FEEL IT. She was squirming and writhing and moaning like I was a goddess.

—MICHELLE, 41

Lips

Lips are soft and supple and incredibly versatile. Use them for kissing, sucking, pinching, humming—all of these are great tricks of the trade. Open or closed, there are plenty of ways to use your lips.

- Cover her with light kisses from her perineum on up. Kiss her pussy lips the way you would the ones on her face—imagine that's what you're doing and really get into it.

- Wrap your lips around your teeth and pull the skin of her inner lips into your mouth, pinching and licking as you go.

- Open your mouth wide and place it on top of her

vulva, slowly closing your lips around it while suck-ing it away from her body and quickly flicking her lips with your tongue.

🍒 Take her clit into your mouth as if it were an oyster on a shell. Suck it, pull on it, and let it slide through your lips. Repeat this over and over. Wrap your lips around your teeth and take her clit into your mouth, biting down and pinching as you pull her clit away from her body.

🍒 Roll her clit between your lips; hum while you do this and add a little vibration to the process.

🍒 Take her whole mound into your mouth, lower lip in her vagina, and close your mouth over it, licking her clit as you go.

Fingers

I've always thought food tastes a lot better if you eat it with your fingers. There's something so much more sensuous and decadent about it, and the same goes for eating pussy. Having your fingers, mouth, and tongue all going at it at the same time is incredibly hot for both of you. Sticking your fingers inside her vagina and fucking away while licking and sucking her clit gives her the best of both worlds.

- Run your fingers through her pubic hair and tug lightly while you lap at her labia.
- Tickle and pinch her perineum.
- Slide your fingers all the way into her vagina and press on her G-spot while your tongue pushes against the outer wall on her mound.
- Stick your thumb up her cunt and your finger up her asshole while nibbling on her clit.
- Stroke her entire vulva with your finger, then lick it, over and over. Penetrate her at the end of each finger stroke as well.
- Rub circles on her clit with the pads of your fingers while you tongue her vagina. Press down on her mound, tweak her nipples, or squeeze her ass while you eat her out.
- Slide your hands under her ass and press her pussy into your face. Slip your thumbs up her ass crack and massage either side of her vulva while you do this. Another version is to fuck her with your thumbs while you press her into you. Slide her pussy up and down your face with your hands and really get in there.

Fingering Note: Fingers are also great to tide her over while you give your tongue a rest. Taking a break while she's totally into it can be a large bummer, so use your fingers to keep her hot and bothered while you let your face muscles recharge.

Teeth

Little nibbles down there can be incredibly exciting as long as you don't bite down too hard. This isn't for everyone; pay close attention and make sure she's into it before you get carried away.

- 🍒 Take her inner labia between your teeth and tug on them. Softly nibble on them while you lick the edges with your tongue.
- 🍒 Nibble on her outer labia, perineum, and thighs.
- 🍒 If she can handle it, pull her clit between your teeth and give it a little love bite.

Face Plant

Along with all its fabulous, separate parts, your face as a whole is a great giver of oral pleasure. If you really get in there and ram your whole face in, it'll provide a lot more pressure than just your tongue or your fingers can. Which is quite a plus, since we all know how great a lot of pressure feels.

- Rub your nose back and forth across her clit. Use it to press down on her clit or her mound while you munch on her vulva.
- Nod your head "yes" and "no" while you rub your nose, mouth, and chin over her whole pussy. Keep your tongue out and pointed while you do this.
- Do nice, long, fat, lazy licks with your tongue, up and down and side to side, while you press in hard.

Face Plant Note: With your whole face in there, it can get a little hard to breathe, so take a big gulp of air before heading in. Another option is to keep pressing hard with a flat tongue while you tip your head back for a breather.

All of these techniques are valuable, because different women like different things, and some like certain things more than others. In order to get an idea of what the most popular techniques are, I polled a bunch of women on their all-time favorite things to have done to them while getting their salads tossed. Obviously it's the combination of moves, textures, speeds, and pressures that makes for a good time, but when pressed, everyone was able to choose one thing above the rest. The pie chart below illustrates the answers to the following question:

If somebody shot you while you were getting eaten out,

what would be the last sensation you'd want to feel on your pussy before you died—flat tongue, pointed tongue, clit-suck, humming, pinching, fingering, or face plant?

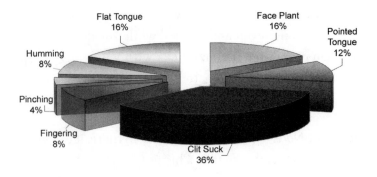

PUSSY EATING PIE CHART

Positions

Along with various tools and techniques, accessing her pussy from different directions can also increase her pleasure. Experiment with as many positions as you can think of to see which ones work best for you. Here are a few ideas to get you started:

STANDARD FARE

The standard, meat-and-potatoes version where she lies on her back and you slide, face down, between her legs is always a crowd pleaser. You can vary it by putting her legs over your shoulders or having her pull her knees up to her chest.

vocabulary builder

PILLOW QUEEN:
a woman who sits back and lets her
lover do all the work

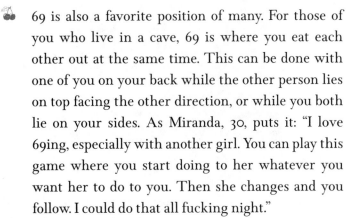

69 is also a favorite position of many. For those of you who live in a cave, 69 is where you eat each other out at the same time. This can be done with one of you on your back while the other person lies on top facing the other direction, or while you both lie on your sides. As Miranda, 30, puts it: "I love 69ing, especially with another girl. You can play this game where you start doing to her whatever you want her to do to you. Then she changes and you follow. I could do that all fucking night."

Try sliding her to the edge of the bed while you sit on the floor. She puts her legs over your shoulders and rests her heels on your back. It's as if you're sitting at the table and she's the main course. This can be done in chairs and on countertops and stuff too. This position is especially great for using your fingers or toys, since you have such easy access and

SITTING DOWN TO EAT

you're sitting up. It's also great if you've got a bathtub with a big enough rim around it for her to sit on the side. You can eat her out and trickle water on her at the same time.

Then there's the ever-popular shut-up-and-sit-on-my-face version. This is great because she's in control of how intense the pressure is, making it one of the most interactive positions out there. It's nice if there's a headboard she can grab, to adjust her weight. Otherwise she can vary the pressure with her leg muscles, which gives her a little less control but a better workout. If someone's sitting on your face and really going for the grind, lots of licking and opening and closing of your mouth makes for nice friction.

🍒 Another favorite is the somewhat dominant/submissive version where one person kneels down and munches while the other remains standing. This is fun if you both start fully clothed and the eater slowly strips the eatee.

> I love being at a party and running into the bathroom, whipping down her pants, getting on my knees, and going at it right there. All the better if I can hear people talking right outside the door.
>
> —JANE, 23

🍒 There's also a rather gymnastic, yoga-esque position that basically has her doing a shoulder stand in your face. You kneel up on the bed and she's upside-down with her back to you, with the back of her neck and shoulders on the bed, her feet over your shoulders

SHOULDER STAND

or on the wall behind you. Pull her into you until her pussy is right below your chin and then dive in. This gives you great access and also puts gravity on your side.

Try having her get on all fours while you slide underneath, checking her hood. To avoid a wicked neck cramp, use some pillows to hold your head up, or have her drop down a bit.

I like the sideways-pussy-eating thing. This is more light fare, more teasing kind of stuff because you can't

*really get in there. Your bodies are perpendicular; she's
on her side with one leg straight on the bed and the other
bent with her foot on the bed. You're using her straight
leg as a pillow and going at her sideways, like you're
playing the harmonica. It gives a different sensation because you can't really get in there so hard–it makes you
do it a little lighter, which is nice for variety.*

–Amy, 34

Side Dishes

Another way to add to the fun is to bring in some outside
help. Put things like ice cubes or cough drops in your
mouth before you go down on her and let her experience
the different temperatures and sensations. Hold the ice
cube in your lips and rub it over her vulva. Stick it in her
pussy and suck it out. Keep it in your mouth while you're
licking her and let the cold water spill out over her pussy.
Vary the sensation by putting hot tea in your mouth, heating up your tongue and lips, and then going back for more.
Mentholated cough drops can add zing to both your mouth
and her pussy. Rub it on her vulva and stick it inside her,
really working her with your tongue to get it out. (Make
sure the cough-drops or anything else you put inside her is

sugar-free—sugar can feed a nasty yeast infection.)

Toys also make nice additions to eating her out. Rub a vibrator on her clit while you munch her vulva. Press a vibrator against or inside her asshole. Fuck her with a dildo in her pussy or her ass while you suck on her clit. (See the following chapter for more info on how to bring toys into the game.)

Like all things sex, eating pussy is about enthusiasm, consideration, and communication. Whether or not you wind up liking it, trying it will make you that much more sexually well-rounded, which is never a bad thing. Personally, I'm not a huge fan of eating out, but I wasn't freaked out by it either. I'm really glad to have done it and to know a little about what it must feel like to go down on me. Even though it wasn't the thing I'd get excited to do the most, seeing how much pleasure it gave her was great. But that's just me. I don't like getting eaten out very much, either, so what the hell do I know? Everybody's different, and for all you know eating pussy could turn out to be something you like and are really good at. So get in there and find out.

See, that wasn't so bad, was it?

chapter six

Pandora's Toybox: Advanced Gettin' Some

Sex toys and girls just go together. I sometimes use them with men but I tend to use them more regularly with women. I don't know why. Maybe women are more open. Or maybe we just have more holes.

—LESLIE, 35

One of the excellent things about the modern world is that there are sex toys. Tons and tons and tons of them. And there's also the Internet, meaning that no matter where you live, if you have access to a computer and a credit card you can buy something to play with. I love my sex toys. I love going to sex stores and browsing around, seeing what new things I can slide inside myself or strap my latest lover to. There's a plethora of toys available today, in enough shapes and sizes to make your head spin, so whatever it is you desire to do—tweak, screw, pinch, whip, vibrate, plug, tease, blind, bind, gag, spank, suck, schtupp—there's sure to be a device out there to help you do it.

When you're getting it on with a chick, toys can add a hot and sexy edge to an already hot and sexy situation. But in any kind of partner sex, as well as in masturbation, toys are more of a bonus prize, rather than an essential part of the act. And they're not for everybody. Some people like to feel everything that's going on, so sticking something like a dildo, rather than their own finger or tongue, up their lover's hoo seems like a rip-off because they can't feel it. Some people don't like the way sex toys feel or can't get off knowing something foreign is doing all the work. And some people are just too plain lazy to haul them out, lube them up, and clean them off. I know I've certainly opted for more standard fare on many an occasion when the toys seemed to be just too much damn work. But I give them an enthusiastic two thumbs up, and so do plenty of other people, making the adult toy industry a rapidly expanding one that gets more and more creative every year.

There are infinite ways to use toys and have sex in general, some of which require a little planning and others that are more spontaneous. If you decide to, say, tie your babe up to the four corners of your bed, blindfold her, torture her with a feather, finger her to the point of coming, pull away just in time, and then finish her off with the strap-on, you could orchestrate an evening around that scenario. You could rig the bed with the necessary hooks and ropes ahead of time, get all your toys cleaned and ready, and crank the heat so when she's lying there naked she doesn't freeze her tits off. Planning stuff out and blowing her mind with your dirty little surprises makes for a totally fun date, and I highly recommend taking the time to do it if you find yourself in the right situation.

But never stick to a step-by-step agenda. Like I said before, sex is instinctive; always trust yourself and go with the flow. If you go about it like "First I will squeeze her nipple and then I will stick my finger in her pussy and then I will pull it in and out and then I will lick it," chances are you won't be so hot. Knowledge can sometimes get in the way of what comes naturally, so let yourself go and really feel what you're doing. The best way to be a good lay, no matter who you're sleeping with, is simply to be turned on, to really want to fuck that person well and to really want that person all over you. All the tricks and toys in the world won't help you if you're not into it. So don't think of these chapters as instruction manuals; think of them as a reference library where you store your ideas until you need them.

Let's Go Shopping!

If you decide to go the toy route, knowing what to buy can be tough since you can't really tell what will suit you until you test it out. Unfortunately (or fortunately, I guess) sex shops don't provide you with testers, so you pretty much have to make an educated guess and pray for the best. Which can get pricey, since you can't exactly go into a store and exchange the dildo you bought yesterday for the next size up after a long evening of not finding it satisfying enough. But there are reviews you can read, friends you can ask, and books, websites, and videos that cover all the details (see the back of the book for suggestions). These are especially helpful for those of you who live somewhere where there are no sex stores. Since you're really shooting in the dark, the more reading up on the topic you can do the better. I also recommend buying the cheapest thing out there just to see if you like using toys at all. Prices vary considerably, and it's a good idea to try out something like a cheapo rubber dildo before dropping a wad on a fancy silicone one.

If you live in the vicinity of a sex store, you're in much better shape, although going to a store and buying sex toys can be a tad awkward because it's such a personal thing. Holding up two dildos to see which is bigger may not be the kind of thing you'd like to do in front of an entire store full of strangers. Plus a lot of sex stores have a super-sleazy vibe, complete with jerk-off booths and a creepy guy behind the counter—not exactly the kind of place you want to let it all hang out. For a long time sex shops were pretty much all like that, but thankfully, in the past two decades or so, a slew of excellent sex-positive stores have opened up and completely changed the whole scenario. Most of them are woman-owned and have a more nurturing vibe. They hire friendly, educated people who can pretty much answer any questions you have and who will make you feel like a superhero for tending to your lustful needs. Many of these stores set out samples of their various products so you can gauge the size or vibrational power and get a feel for the material. Some also offer a wide range of sex workshops as well as sell a great selection of books. They are a joy and give me great hope for the sexual liberation of our poor, repressed human race! Check out the back of this book for a list of fabulous stores around the country.

My first sex toy was a purple Slimline vibrator (a six-inchish-long plastic vibrating thing shaped like a giant bullet) that I got when I moved to New York right after college. I didn't really know what I wanted, other than something I could stick inside myself, and I wasn't too sure about the vibrating part, but I was curious. I figured since this thing was the right shape and it vibrated I could kill two birds with one stone. As it turned out I never really used the damn thing. It ended up being too slim to really satisfy my penetration needs (duh, it's called the Slimline) and the vibrations made my vagina go numb. I had no idea that those things are mostly meant to be used on your clit, rather than for penetration.

For years afterward, even though I spent many a paycheck on other types of sex toys, I steered clear of vibrators. In fact it's only been very recently that I climbed aboard the vibrator bandwagon. After the Slimline debacle I'd periodically test out different kinds but the vibration was always too intense on my clit. It was too distracting and kind of hurt. It wasn't until I got a vibrating rubber ducky that I saw the light. It's nothing fancy, just has the one speed, but the vibration is the perfect intensity for me *and* I can take him in the bathtub because he's waterproof. He fits me perfectly: his little rubber ducky head presses right into my clit and his pointy little tail hits me right on my butthole. I can even leave him out in plain sight, 'cuz nobody knows what he is. It's just a matter of getting past the whole Ernie-and-Bert thing.

My issues aside, the majority of women really respond to vibration down there, thanks to our clitoral pal and her 8,000 nerve endings, We just love stuff like riding on trains, sitting on washing machines, and cramming our cell phones down deep into our pockets. I know plenty of women who can get off by sticking vibrators inside themselves as well—with any of these toys, you can obviously do whatever the hell you want with them as long as you don't harm yourself. Or the toy. And if you're one of those people who doesn't get off on vibrators at all, you're just one of those people who doesn't get off on vibrators. There's nothing wrong with you. You excel in other areas. And there are more than enough other toys to choose from.

The following is a very brief overview of all the stuff that's been made with your sexual pleasure in mind, plus some tips on how to use it. What I cover is just the very tippy-top of the iceberg; there are countless options, in all sizes, shapes, materials, and colors. For a more thorough understanding of what's available, I highly recommend going to your nearest sex shop and seeing all there is to see. They've come up with so many things to do to your various body parts it's staggering. Some items are just ha-ha novelties and some are really useful. It's sometimes hard to tell which is which. I recently saw a giant inflatable ball with a dildo attached to it—I guess you sit on the ball and hop around while fucking yourself. I'm not sure which category that falls in.

vocabulary builder

RIDING FOR FREE:
When an everyday activity
provides genital stimulation,
i.e., going horseback riding,
sitting on a subway seat.

Vibrators

In general, there are two kinds of vibrators—the kind that plug into the wall and the battery-operated kind. The main difference between the two is that the plug-in kind tend to be a lot more powerful and can run as long as your electric bill's paid, so if you need steady, heavy, brute-strength vibration, these are the ones for you. The downsides are you need to be near an outlet and you can't use them in water. Battery-operated vibrators are much more portable and range from the teeny and discreet to the mighty and well-hung. There's been some seriously creative thinking going on in this arena—you can find battery-powered vibrators that are waterproof, that strap on to a penis or dildo, that you wear on your finger, that move around inside you AND stroke your clit . . . they even make some that you can strap to your twat and wear all day long.

Another consideration is noise. Different vibrators make different amounts of noise, so if you live in a small house with roommates or can't concentrate with the buzzing noise, get a quiet one. Go to a sex shop and listen to what their vibrators sound like. If the store doesn't have any display models for you to check out, ask the person behind the counter if they'd mind opening one up for you. If you can't get to a store, call one and ask someone to help you make your choice. I realize discussing your purchase with a total stranger might be difficult, but keep in mind that the people who work in these places have seen a lot. I can't imagine anything you could dish out would faze them in the least. You can also look for stuff online. The better websites give you a noise rating.

Vibrators come in a variety of materials, as well. Silicone is the best as it's smooth, durable, nonporous (easy to clean), and retains body heat. Jelly rubber feels great but is porous so it can get slimy and is hard to clean. Metal and hard plastic are easy to clean and have more intense vibrating power since none of the action is being absorbed by a soft, rubbery layer.

Whatever kind of vibrational experience you're after, there's sure to be something out there that'll get you off; you may just have to go through a bit of trial and error before hitting the jackpot.

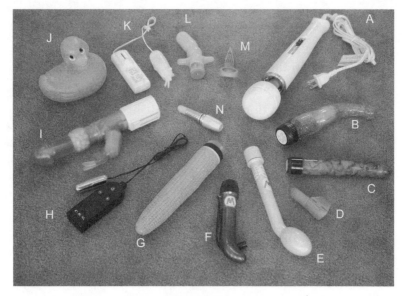

VIBRATORS

(A) HITACHI MAGIC WAND (B) JUDY JETSON RUBBER VIBE W/G-SPOT CURVE (C) GIDGET WATERPROOF HARD PLASTIC VIBE (D) FOKUOKU SLIP-ON-YER-FINGER VIBE (E) G-EGG LONG PLASTIC G-SPOT STIMULATOR (F) STUBBY HARD PLASTIC VIBE WITH G-SPOT CURVE (G) CORN ON THE COB (H) BULLET VIBE (I) RABBIT PEARL (A FAVORITE AMONG MASTURBATORS) (J) RUB MY DUCKIE WATERPROOF PLASTIC VIBE (K) HONEY BEAR (L) STUBBY TUBBY WATERPROOF HARD PLASTIC G-SPOT VIBE (M) HONEY SPOT RUBBER COCK OR DILDO RING WITH TEXTURED VIBRATING CLIT NUB (N) LIPSTICK VIBE

WHAT VIBRATORS AND DILDOS ARE MADE OF

	PROS	CONS
RUBBER	One of the cheapest options out there Comes in a massive variety of shapes, sizes, textures, and colors Can be found every-where sex toys are sold	Very porous, which makes it super-greasy and hard to keep clean Hard to keep lint and cat hair from sticking to it Can get tears and rips Can have a rubbery smell
SILICONE	Most popular material among those in the know (who can afford it) Lasts forever Nonporous, which makes it easy to clean Nice solid texture Absorbs body heat and vibration	Expensive Not as wide a variety available as other ma-terials Can be hard to find in low-rent sex shops Can't be used with sili-cone lube (breaks it down and makes it all sticky and funky)

	PROS	CONS
PLASTIC	Nonporous, which makes it easy to clean Cheap Slick, smooth feel (Vibrators) Vibration can be super-intense due to lack of rubber or silicone padding between vibrating mechanism and your body	Can be chintzy and easy to break (Vibrators) Vibration can be too intense due to lack of rubber or silicone padding between vibrating mechanism and your body
GLASS (dildos)	Smooth and hard and lovely Easy to clean Many are beautiful, handblown works of art	Usually super-expensive Hard to find Not a wide variety of options

Battery-Powered Vibrators

The Bullet Family

Bullet vibrators are little and orb-like and usually made out of hard plastic. They come in several forms—as stand-alone orbs, as orbs housed in some sort of outer casing, or as orbs attached by a cord to a small battery pack with a bunch of controls on it. With the latter, the idea is to press the orb against whichever body part you want to feel the vibration on, and adjust the intensity with the controls. If the vibration, even on the lowest setting, is too intense, they make these rubber sleeves you can put on the orb to absorb some of the buzz. The sleeves come in a ton of colors and are usually shaped like little rabbits or bears or something, which is weird, but as long as they're not shaped like my father I don't care what the fuck they look like. They are sold separately and can be used on a whole bunch of different vibrators depending on their size.

How to Use Them: Because of its wee size, the bullet is easily incorporated into almost any kind of play. Putting a dab of lube on the bullet and rubbing it around her pussy while you make out is a nice way to get things going. Try using it while you're fingering her, pressing down on her clit with the bullet in the palm of your hand while you send your fingers into her vagina. This you can do lying side by side or with her back to your chest while you reach around and grab her from behind. You can use a bullet while you eat her out too, holding it on her clit or rubbing it around her vagina. Try working up to it, licking and sucking her first and then bringing in the bullet, rolling it around with your tongue while you lick her, pressing it into her vagina while you suck on her clit (be careful not to let the vibrator touch your teeth—it feels awful). The only place a bullet should never wander is inside anyone's butt-hole, because your sphincter may decide not to let it out.

Wiener-Shaped Vibrators

Unlike the unassuming shape of the bullet, some vibrators have shapes that seem to scream "Stick it on in thar!" Whether you use these kinds of vibrators internally, externally, or both is up to you. If the realistic-penis look doesn't do it for you, you can find a vibrator shaped like such things as a dolphin, a woman, or a vegetable. They also vary in vibrational oomph and number of speed settings. Some vibrators have a bendable spine inside so you can change the shape to go straight in, to hit your G-spot, or whatever you want. If you're really looking for a party, they also make some that glow in the dark, light up like a dance floor, or have weird Lava Lamp type ooze inside them.

Other specialty items to keep your eye out for are curved vibrators whose only care in the world is poking and massaging your G-spot. And if you want a butt buzz, there are special probelike versions and ones curved to access your G-spot through the back door.

How to use them: Wiener-shaped vibrators are nice because there are a couple of ways to use them: you can use them as a dildo without turning them on, use them as a vibrating dildo, or use them externally. One way is to start by laying her on her back and kneeling next to her. Tease her with the vibrator, gently rubbing it around her pussy, poking a teeny bit into her vagina, with the power off. Slowly start to move it in and out of her vagina while you play with her nipples and kiss her. Then turn it on, pulling it in and out, running it slowly along her clit on its way deep inside her vagina and then back out again, over and over. Flip her over onto her stomach and have her squeeze her legs together. Put some lube on the vibrator and slide it down her butt crack and along her pussy. Pull it in and out while you reach one hand beneath her and massage her clit. Eventually slide the vibrator beneath her clit and lie on top of her back while both of you grind down into the bed.

Waterproof vibrators

Water and girl-on-girl sex go hand in hand. I like doing chicks in water because it's so sensual, I love rubbing soap all over each other and getting all slippery and wet and stuff. If you bring a waterproof vibrator in with you, that can make it even better.

How to use them: Dribble water on her clit with your mouth while you massage her vulva with the vibrator. Push her pussy down underwater with the vibrator while you soap up her tits. If you have a glass or plastic dildo, rub that over her pussy underwater while you vibe her asshole.

Party in your pants

As if hand-held vibrators weren't sublime enough, some genius came up with the idea to make a vibrator that you can strap onto your body like a happy pair of panties. This means that not only are your hands free to molest you or whoever you happen to be with, but that you can wear it out, like to work and stuff. How great is that? These wearable vibrators come in different sizes, shapes, and colors. They make some that fit over your whole situation, from vagina to butthole, and others that fit snugly over just your clitoral area, making them ideal accompaniments to penetration. The most popular one is shaped like a butterfly and is deceptively called a Butterfly Vibrator. They also make these panty things with a little pouch in front that you can slide a teeny-tiny bullet or other small vibrator into.

How to use them: These are as fun to wear outside the house as they are to wear in the bedroom. Strapping one on before going out with your girl can drive you both wild with anticipation. And if you're going out alone and are on the prowl, wearing one can up your confidence and make you more assertive about hooking up with someone. If you're using a strap-on vibrator during sex, try putting it on your girl nice and slowly, making that part of the play. Slide it slowly up each leg while you face each other standing. Hold it in place against her clit while you turn it on and kiss her. Slowly lay her down on the bed and straddle her crotch, you sitting upright with your back facing her. Position yourself over the vibrator so you reap some of the benefits as well while you finger her. If the vibrator is one that only covers her clit, using a dildo instead of your fingers can be great, too.

> My girlfriend and I love wearing our butterflies out to clubs. It's like we have this dirty little secret and are so turned on we can't wait to get home and fuck. Actually, we usually don't wait, we usually wind up going at it in the bathroom!
>
> —HILARY, 21

Miscellaneous

There are all sorts of attachments and various types of sleeves you can add on to certain vibrators to change the texture, diminish the vibration, or allow them to hit you in a different spot. If your vibrator's buzzing is too intense for you, you can wrap it in a towel or put a pillow between it and you. To spice up a dildo or add more buzz to a vibrator, there are little vibrators attached to rings that you can slide right on to your toy. Another interesting option is the Five Finger Fantasy, a magical glove with five vibrating fingers. There's even software now that turns your cell phone into a sex toy by making it vibrate on command.

Electric Vibrators

Wands

Big, loud, durable, and hands-down the most powerful vibrators there are, wands do not fuck around. At all. There are several brands to chose from, but the Hitachi Magic Wand is the one everyone talks about. It's a solid foot long, with a tennis-ball-sized vibrating head that has changed the lives of thousands upon thousands of women. It features two no-nonsense speeds and can be used with a number of attachments should you desire some penetration to go with your vibes.

How to use them: Because wands are so powerful and practically indestructible, they can be great accompaniments to humping. Lie on top of her and slide the vibrator between you so it's pressing on both your clits while you grind away. If the head of the vibe is uncomfortable or too hard to keep in place, wrap it in a towel. You can hump lying on top of each other, standing up against the wall, or with her sitting in a chair while you straddle her. This last way will have the vibe working her clit while it massages your butthole.

Coil vibrators

Gentler and less imposing than the wands, coil vibrators are loved by many for their smaller heads, quicker vibes, and virtually silent buzz. Coils usually come with several different attachments of varied textures to be used for external massages. Attachments are available for penetration as well. Whatever you do, don't take electric vibrators into the bathtub or shower, or you will die.

How to use them: While having someone press an electric vibrator onto your clit can be orgasmic, don't forget that a vibrator can relieve stress on backs and shoulders and other wholesome places. After all, this is, as any good Christian person will tell you, what vibrating massagers were made for. While you're fingering her or fucking her with a dildo, massage her neck and back with the vibrator. Another doozy is to pinch her nipples while you hold a vibrator against them. It's kind of hard to maneuver but feels great.

Dildos

Another staple no sex toy collection should be without is a really good dildo. Dildos add an extra bang to masturbation and can offer a whole new dimension to your sex life with other women. The only problem is figuring out which one, or ones, to get. I bet if you lined up every single kind of dildo for sale in the world, tips to balls, you could make it halfway across the United States. I think what my father would say about dildos is this: "You people these days, you have so many choices you get stuck. It's like a little child in a candy store who can have anything she wants. She is so excited by all her options she can't decide, and soon the store is closed and she has nothing. The child who could only have a lollipop has her lollipop and is happy with it." What Dad is saying here is that we are spoiled, and that in his day you got your dildo and it was the dildo you got and that was that. What he doesn't realize is that if you do a little thinking and narrow down your options a bit before you visit the candy store, you can get out of there before it closes, and take home something much better than a lollipop.

The most important consideration when buying a dildo is size. If you've never stuck anything inside yourself, you're just going to have to wing it, but if you know what you like, you're in good shape. If it's too hard for you to just eyeball the selections in the store, measure your boyfriend's cock and go from there. Or next time you discover that the cucumber you just stuck inside yourself is perfect, get out the tape measure. Dildos come in every size and shape, from skinny little Needledick-the-Bug-Fucker types to something that looks like a fire hydrant, and everything in between.

The second most important consideration is texture. Refer to the chart on pages 155–56 to see which material suits you best. And remember, although it's a good idea to get the best quality you can afford, if you're not sure what size or shape you want, try out the cheap stuff first and lay down the real cash once you know what really works for you.

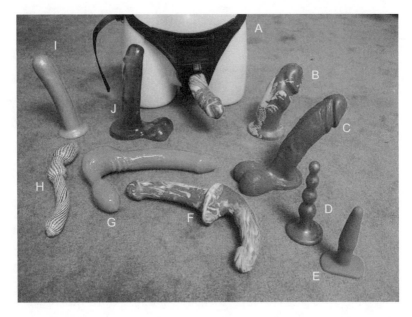

DILDOS

(A) STRAP-ON HARNESS AND DILDO (B) BIG MAMA DILDO (C) REALISTIC COCK AND
BALLS (D) RIPPLE BUTT PLUG (E) NONSKID BUTT PLUG (F) NEXUS DOUBLE-SIDED
DILDO (G) FEELDOE DOUBLE DILDO (H) HAND-BLOWN GLASS DILDO (I) SILK
SILICONE DILDO(J)) JELLY JAMMIN' RUBBER DILDO

The Specifics

Even after you've decided on size and material, you've only
just begun. The best way to figure out the details is to
think about what you'll mostly be using your dildo for.

Most people multitask, using the same dildo for masturbation, partner sex, both anal and vaginal penetration, and so on. If you've always fantasized about fucking a chick with a double-sided dildo, for instance, but also need something to masturbate with, get the double-sided and use it for both. Double-sideds come in a multitude of shapes and sizes. On good ones, one end is straight and the other curved to better fit two bodies that are facing each other. Some have bumps on one head and are smooth on the other and some are textured on both ends.

> My girlfriend had this double-sided dildo that was like a spine and it would stay in whatever position we bent it in. We'd put it in the shape of a V at just the right angle so we could fuck each other. It was hot!
>
> —KENDRA, 33

If it's strap-on sex you crave, you'll need to get a dildo with a wide flat base or balls on it to hold it in the harness. Do you want it to look like a real live penis with head, veins, and balls, or would you prefer a dolphin? Do you want it textured with bumps and ridges, or do you like it smooth? If you like to keep the action hands-free, get a dildo with a suction cup on the end—you can stick it to a counter or a bathtub and ride away. If you want one that doubles as a vibrator, there are some with holes in the base that you can slide a bullet or some other small vibrator into. If you're looking for G-spot stimulation, get one with the tell-tale curve. Some people want a dildo that has a big head and a thinner shaft, some like it the other way around, and some like uniform width all the way along. They also make dildos shaped like fists.

Just a little thought before you head out will make it easier to decide. Because there's such a wide range of uses for these fabulous items, most people who like them have more than one in their collections. Here are some of the fun things you can do with a hot chick and a dildo.

Fingering

Rubbing her clit, fingering her butthole, tugging at her nipples, pulling her hair—all of these are great in combination with dildo and vibrator play. One of my favorites is to stack up a bunch of pillows and put them under her hips while she lies on her stomach. Kneel next to her, spread her legs, and tease her with the dildo while you rub her body (it's nice to lie on the dildo or stick it between your thighs to warm it up first). Slowly start putting it in and, while you're fucking her, rub her clit with your other hand. Putting a dab of lube on your fingers before circling her clit can make it all that much more luscious. It's also nice to reach down and rub a vibrator on her clit while you're penetrating her.

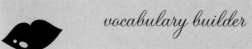

vocabulary builder

CARPOOLING:
when two people ride the same double-sided dildo at the same time

Dual Penetration

Using a double-sided dildo was one thing I fantasized about a lot before I actually got together with a chick. It just seemed so hot to both be getting penetrated at the same time—and lo and behold, 'tis true! I have a crappy double-sided dildo: it's super-bendy, but it's too skinny and it's always popping out of me or the other girl. I recommend getting one made out of silicone that holds its shape, or one with an internal spine that you can adjust. You can hump with a dildo inside both your vaginas, one vagina and one butthole, or two buttholes—all are met with applause. You can vary your positions, too. Try using a double-sided dildo while you lie on top of her, grinding your clits together while you fuck. The scissors position is also great, where you sit or lie with your legs scissored around each other and your pussies sealed together, each getting penetrated at the same time. You can also climb on her back and do it doggy style. Then there's the whole butt-to-butt double-sided dildo thing (where you're both on all fours with your asses pressing up against each other). For this you need a straight dildo rather than a curved one. It's nice to finger yourself at the same time, or, if you can reach, finger each other.

Eating Pussy

After you get her all warmed up with your mouth, start teasing her with a dildo. Start by pressing it against the opening of her vagina and her clit and tease her while you lick, not putting it in right away. Then slowly slide it inside her while you continue to lick and suck her clit. Try licking the area around her vagina while you slide it in and out. It's nice to switch off, too: fuck her with the dildo while you suck her clit, and then just use your mouth, reintroducing the dildo after a couple of minutes to make it more like a treat.

Many of the same tricks can be done to her butthole as well. Just adding pressure from a dildo on her butthole while you eat her out is awesome. If you're going to penetrate her, make sure to go slowly and use lots of lube. Then slide the dildo in and out while you go down on her and watch her go through the roof.

Strap-Ons

I think putting a dildo in a harness and strapping it to your body is so exhilarating. You feel powerful, sexy, and kind of like a big ol' freak. It's this last part that makes me feel that strap-ons deserve special mention here. For me, feeling a little freaky is a huge turn on, but I realize that looking down your body, past your breasts and curves, and seeing this erect penis bouncing out of your crotch may be a little more gender bending than some of you signed up for. If this is the case, I suggest starting out on the receiving end a few times before strapping it on yourself. Enjoying sex as the recipient might be a little less intimidating and will get you used to seeing a strap-on on a woman. Especially if she feels hot and sexy and wields it with confidence; it can help you wrap your brain around how it might be a fun, sexy experience for you.

If it's the actual penis-ness of it all that bothers you, try getting a dildo that's shaped more like a vague phallus rather than one that looks like an actual dick with veins and balls. And if it turns out that strap-ons are just not for you, don't worry about it. There are plenty of other things you can do to have a good time; forcing yourself to do something you're not into is never any fun.

But for those of you who can get into it, strap-on sex is really exhilarating. It's so different from anything you're used to, and it's hot to feel like you've taken a secret peek into the masculine experience. It makes you feel powerful and kinky, and it can make you more comfortable switching the roles around with boys. Here are some other reasons strapping one on rules:

- You get the best of both worlds.
- Unlike hand-held dildos, strap-ons keep your hands free to tend to other body parts.
- If you're wearing it and you position it just so, the back of the dildo presses up against your clit so you get your clitoral jollies too.
- If you're on the receiving end, and you're feeling homesick, you can pretend she's a guy.
- You get a workout.
- You feel like a super stud.
- If you miss sucking cock, you can suck on hers.

- 🍒 You can get your cock sucked.
- 🍒 You already have a wealth of position ideas from getting it on with the boys.
- 🍒 You can come up with new position ideas to take back to the boys.
- 🍒 You expand your sexual know-how just that much more.

> I find that a lot of straight women really like strapping it on and fucking me. I guess it's because they're always on the receiving end with guys. I think it gives them a sense of power—"I'm sick of always being the one that gets fucked, I want to fuck a chick now!"—and it totally gets them off.
>
> —ALICIA, 42

Purchasing Tips

Just to clear up any confusion, a "strap-on" is the combination of the dildo and the harness that you strap the dildo onto your body with. When you're buying one, first consider the kind of harness you want to get. Harnesses generally have a more or less triangular patch in front with a ringed hole in the center (for the dildo to go through) that attaches onto your body with a series of straps. Harnesses come in leather, rubber, vinyl, and nylon, and they vary in price and comfort.

Your harness should fit as snugly as possible so your dildo doesn't slide around and so it feels as much a part of your body as possible. You'll probably have to futz with the straps and the buckles for a while before getting it just right, which is why I highly recommend spending the dough and getting a harness with adjustable straps. You can find cheapo versions that aren't adjustable, but I can't imagine how they work—it can be tricky enough getting the perfect fit when you can move stuff around.

Any decent sex shop will not only let you try the harness on in the store but will also provide a helpful and educated salesperson to show you the ropes. Also, make sure to try out dildos with your harness before buying anything. You may think you'd like having balls on your cock, but a flat-backed dildo might end up feeling better to you. And if you think you might like a little vibrating action, they make harnesses with pouches on them where you can stick a little bullet vibe if you want.

Wearing It Well

Once you get your body fitted to it, it's time to get the rest
of yourself to cooperate. I highly recommend taking a little
time to get used to your new member. Stroke it and play
with it and imagine you can feel everything you're doing
to it. Form a bond with it and try to make it part of your
body. Turn yourself on by jerking it off. Have your lover
suck on it and stroke it. The more a part of *you* your strap-
on feels like, the more connected to it you'll be when it
comes time to penetrate your lover. This will make you
more tuned in to what it's doing and how it's affecting her,
making the experience hotter for both of you.

Another trick is getting your coordination to cooperate. You're going to be using muscles you've never, ever used before, so you're going to have to learn a new rhythm and get yourself in shape. The first time I tried strapping it on I was full of new admiration for men. It was like learning to walk all over again—I had no idea how to access any of those muscles, and when I finally did it was a serious workout! Take your time and find your groove. And don't forget to use your arms if you can. Pumping with your hip muscles is not something women usually do, and it's really awkward. If you're in a position where you can put your body weight on your arms, do so and use them to pull your hips forward. Getting used to the rhythm takes a little practice so don't be alarmed if you feel like you have no control over your body at first.

Once you get acclimated you're ready to go. Here are some fun positions to get you on your way.

🍒 Lie on your back and have her suck your cock while she fingers your clit and plays with your tits. This is a great warmup to get you both hot and bothered and used to the strap-on before the penetration begins.

BLOW JOB

🍒 Lie on your back and have her sit on top of you, with her back facing your head. Have her ride you while she fingers your vagina (which she'll have easy access to, it will be right underneath her crotch).

🍒 Have her lie on her back while you lie on top of her. In this case, the missionary position offers the bonus of two sets of tits to play with and two clits to rub together.

🍒 Have her lie on her back with her legs in the air. You stand over her, bent over, with all four hands and feet on the bed. Straddle her legs and fuck her by bending and straightening your knees.

DOGGY STYLE

🍒 Have her stand next to the bed and bend over, spreading her legs wide. You stand behind her and fuck her from the back, reaching forward to grab her tits or massage her clit.

🍒 Sit her on a countertop and fuck her while you stand up, facing her. Reach around and grab her ass, pulling her into you. Also take advantage of the fact that both of your clits are easily accessible for fingering.

🍒 Lay her on her stomach and put some pillows under her waist. Lie on top of her and fuck her from behind, reaching under to finger her clit and press her body into yours.

> Fucking her with a strap-on was amazing. I felt like a quarterback. I was ramming her like a *dude!* It was awesome. It was weird to not have any feeling in my dick, but it didn't really matter, the thrusting itself was the most intense sensation!
>
> —MICHELLE, 41

Fanny Packin'

Although a lot of toys that go up your hooch can also go up your butt (only ones that can't get lost up there, please), some are made especially with your back door in mind. This usually means the manufacturer has taken care to put a big fat base on the bottom or attach a sturdy cord so the toy doesn't get sucked inside your ass completely.

When putting anything up your ass or hers, the keys to a pleasant experience are (1) lots of lube; and (2) relaxation. Never ram anything up there without working into it first because you can tear something, plus it can hurt. If you slowly work your way up to it, warm up with a finger or two and plenty of lube, anal penetration can be a rockin' good time. Keep in mind that even if it hurts a little at first, it won't hurt all the time. Your butt sometimes just needs to get used to having stuff up there, and once you've worked past that it feels amazing.

Anal Beads

Anal beads are one of the cheapest thrills out there. They're basically just a string of five or so beads, sometimes increasing in size and sometimes all the same, that you pop one by one into your butt or someone else's. You can do it quickly or savor the feeling, letting the butthole wrap itself around the string before being fed the next bead. Once inside they put exciting pressure on the sensitive anal walls.

Try using anal beads while you're eating her out. Slowly pop them in one by one while you lick her pussy, letting them hang out there for the duration of your play and waiting until she's orgasming to slowly pull them out.

The combination of anal stimulation and a good strong orgasm can be incredible!

Butt Plugs

Butt plugs range in length and girth, from plugs that are skinny and cute to things that can make your eyes go wide with terror. Like anal beads, butt plugs are just as much about hanging out in your ass as they are about going in and coming out. Most of them are tapered—they start out small and slide their way to bigger things before coming to rest at the neck. They come in all sorts of shapes, including some that look like spheres stacked on top of each other for a repeated opening and closing of the sphincter muscles.

Butt plugs are great to keep up your ass or hers while getting off in other ways. You can reach back and tug on them, twist them, or tilt them in different directions while you're working a different part of her body. Keep an eye out for plugs that are specially curved to hit your G-spot through the anal wall as well. If you want to try having anal sex, where you're giving her butthole the old in/out, you'll want to use a dildo, not a butt plug. Butt plugs are made for gradual sticking in and pulling out since most of them have a sort of wide shelf before you reach the neck.

Going back and forth over that quickly, the way you do when you're fucking, could cause some serious damage. A dildo is mostly of a uniform width and is made for quick in-and-out penetration. Just make sure it has a wide base so you don't lose it.

If you'd like some vibration with all this, some butt plugs have a special opening on the bottom where you can stick a little vibrator. Or you can buy a vibrator specially made for rear entry. There are long, ribbed probelike ones and shorter stubby ones. Many of these rotate as well as vibrate.

Anal Note: Keep in mind that it's always a good idea to have a conversation about anal play before springing it on someone. It's the kind of thing that many people aren't too comfy with, and a little conversation beforehand might save some embarrassment.

Doing the Dishes

Taking care to clean your toys properly will not only make them last longer but will keep you from getting any weird cooties from lingering microbes. Dildos, butt plugs, and vibrators should be washed with warm water and antibacterial soap after use. With vibrators that aren't waterproof, make sure not to get water into the battery packs or electrical connections or they will die a quick death. The cyberskin toys need to get a rub down with cornstarch after their baths to retain their lifelike feel. Sex stores sell products specially made for the cleaning and care of your toys. And—I just can't say it enough—use condoms! They make sex all so much damn safer and will cut down on your clean-up time. Especially if you're using rubber toys rather than silicone.

BDSM Lite

BDSM (bondage, domination, sadomasochism) and the toys that go with it often conjure up images of dungeons and welts and scary, unsmiling women dressed in latex and stiletto-heeled boots. BDSM can be any or all of these, or it can be you simply getting eaten out with a blindfold on. How far you want to take it is up to you, the most important thing always being that you do it safely. The world of BDSM is a vast and complex one. My version here is more like BDSM Lite. I'm just going to give you a starter kit of some of the toys you can use to push your sexual play into the red zone. If you want to go deep into it, there are more suggestions in the back of the book.

Regardless of how hardcore you get, the main ingredients for a good BDSM time are trust, communication, and creativity. Trust is key, since it's highly likely that at some point you'll be rendered helpless. It would suck to find out the person you're with is a psycho when they've got you tied to the bed and are screwing nipple clamps to your clit. Communication is vital, because you may be playing with pain or humiliation and it stops being fun when someone gets hurt really badly. And the last ingredient, creativity, is important because a lot of BDSM involves one person doing stuff to another person. If you have no ideas, your poor partner will just be lying there at your incompetent mercy.

Tie 'er up!

One of my personal favorites, tying someone down or being tied up myself, is all about sexual tension and power play. When purchasing restraints, the most important things to look for are comfort, ease getting in and out of them, and of course, how cool they look. They come in leather, nylon, and metal; the better ones have padding or fur on the inside. Most restraints come with D-rings so you can hook them up to your bed, the wall, your torture rack, whatever. If you're using a bed, you can tie a rope around the frame or the headboard and slip it through the

D-rings. This works fine, but as some restraints are kind of a pain in the ass to take on and off, getting some carabiner-type clamps at the hardware store is much better. Tie the rope to the clamps and use them to clip and release the cuffs. This way you can switch out of positions a lot faster. Carabiners are also great for clamping her wrists or ankles together or hogtying her by clamping all four together.

There's something very theatrical about bondage; you're playing out a scene with the bed as a stage and your fantasies as the script. It can really add to the experience if you create an atmosphere—dim the lights, burn some incense, light candles, and make sure to wear something excellent. If that's your play, of course. It's all about anticipation, control, and teasing. When someone can't move, you're completely in control of their pain, their pleasure, and their release. Take your time and drive her crazy with it. Here's an example of the fun you can have.

Tie her wrists to the top of the bed and don't touch her, just tell her all the nasty things you're going to do to her. Leave her lying there by herself to think about it for a while. Put a blindfold on her and slowly run a feather tickler over her body, from her neck down to her pussy. Tease her with your fingers, rub her clit and get her juices flowing and then pull away. Leave the room again. Sneak back in and surprise her with your mouth on her pussy. Strap her ankles to the end of the bed and put a vibrator on the bed near her pussy but not on it. Let her feel the vibrations but don't let her have it yet. Slowly stick your fingers inside her and start fucking her. Take the vibrator and put it on her clit. Lie on top of her and grab her nipples with your teeth. If you have a good setup (with easy-to-remove clamps) you can flip her over easily and get her from behind as well. Use dildos, ice cubes, your tongue, a paddle, whatever you can think of to make this fun. You can also

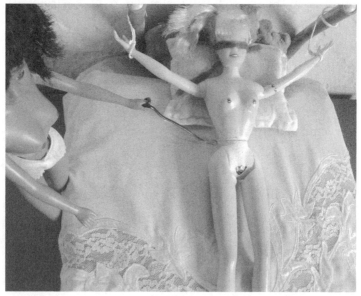

TIED UP

tie someone up less elaborately if you don't have a ton of time. It's nice to sneak her arm into a restraint during sex and just leave her one-armed. Feeling even remotely powerless can be a real turn-on.

Spanking

Every once in a while we all need a good spanking. Luckily there are plenty of devices to help you out. They come in a variety of materials including wood, rubber, and leather, and depending on their size and how flexible they are the sensations will vary. In general, the more give the material has and/or the thinner the object, the more of a smack or a sting it will deliver. If it's a hard thud you're looking for, go with the bigger, sturdier stuff.

Whatever you end up using—a paddle, your hand, a hairbrush, a crop, a wooden spoon, or anything else you can find—test it on yourself first (your leg, your own ass, etc.) to gauge the force so you know what you're dealing with. Be conscious of how hard you're hitting and, above all, communicate with your lover to find out how much she can take. Pay attention to her responses; ask her after the first hit how it felt and gauge your next blow from there. Take it slow and softer at first and give her time to work up to the pain. The harder you hit the more important it is to rub her skin afterward to ease some of the sting. It's nice if you have a furry piece of fabric or an ice cube to rub with as well. Put her over your knee, get her on all fours, lay her on her stomach with some pillows under her hips, and let her have it. Spankings are great for all sorts of things, including role-playing and as a side-dish to penetration or finger fucking; if you do it well, with enough communication, it can really spice things up.

> One of my favorites is having my girl strap it on and push me down on all fours. I love the way she holds my hips and starts out slow, spanking my ass while rubbing my belly and whispering what she's planning on doing to me all night long. Then she'll slap my ass harder and give my hair a tug and start doing me hard and deep.
>
> —TANYA, 29

Public Displays of Affection

Other fun things to investigate on your quest for raunchy sex are sex clubs. On the whole, they're totally seedy and weird but they're also kind of fun. You get to watch people doing all sorts of crazy things, and there's almost always some sort of dungeon-type room where you can pick up some tips to take home. Most major cities have at least one club, and though they're usually really expensive to get into if you're a guy, women are often admitted free. And believe me, if you walk up to a straight club with your chicky and start fooling around, you'll not only get in for free but you'll have a sea of fans once you get in there. If you want to leave the guys out of it completely, some clubs offer all-girl nights too.

Either way, these places can open you up to a whole new world where pretty much anything goes. And for those of you who're having trouble finding a girl to sleep with, sex clubs are ideal places to hook up. Most people who go to these places are pretty open, so your chances of stumbling upon a woman who's up for a little messing around are very good at both the straight and the all-girl clubs. Check your local sex shops, lesbian magazines, and the Internet for information on where to find them.

Porn-O-Rama

Another great way to spice things up is by watching girl-on-girl porn. I think watching people fuck is hot, especially if I'm lucky enough to stumble across a movie where the actresses are sexy and seem turned on by each other. Not an easy feat, but doable, and when it's good it's great—for turning you on, giving you ideas, providing tips, supplying masturbation fodder, and having something hot to watch while you get it on with someone else. You're bound to find something to fit your needs: to say there's a lot to choose from would be an understatement. Not only do the big production houses seem to pump out new movies every second, but there's an ever growing amount of amateur material available. The Internet is also teeming with stuff—there are adult sites that let you stream video, amateur sites where people set up cameras in their bedrooms and let you watch, interactive sites where you can communicate with the person on the screen and have them act out whatever you command, and on and on. All of these cost a minimal fee and come and go on a regular basis, so the best way to find them is to do a search for "lesbian sex" or "lesbian video" or something and you'll be bombarded with options. I recommend a few of the more stable-seeming sites in the back of the book.

As great as porn can be, a couple of upsetting things about it bear mentioning. There's this fun, sexy thing you're watching, and there's the reality that it's probably wreaking psychological havoc on the people acting in it. The same goes for strippers: as hot as I think they are, I can only watch for a while without getting depressed. I realize that the people in the movies and doing the pole dances could be well-adjusted and thrilled with their career choices, and what the fuck do I know, but I can't help feeling a little sad about it.

The other problem is that since we don't spend nearly as much money on porn as men do, the majority of porn is shot by men for men, so there's not much concern with what turns women on. This means that it doesn't matter if the chicks are really getting off as long as you can see their titties and get an eyeful of them eating each other's pussies. For the most part everything's done in outer space, where it can be seen, rather than up close and personal, but when's the last time you made out with someone and you both had your tongues way outside your mouths? You can practically hear the director screaming "Tongues, ladies! We need to see the tongues!" Same goes for pussy eating. Lips are spread wide (with long, scary fingernails) and tongues are flicked delicately, as if the licker is testing the pussy to make sure she won't burn herself on it. Rarely do you see anyone really get in there and mash her pretty face in it. This is because men want to see everything, whereas women want to see what would actually feel good. Yet I think porn like this still has value, because you can pick up on good positions and moves and creative ways to use sex toys, no matter how poorly it's all executed in the movie.

The only way to find out what you like is to get out

there and start watching stuff. A good way to narrow down the field is to ask your friends for suggestions and to check out reviews in books and on websites. I list a bunch of excellent resources in the back of this book, including movies, directors, and porn series I think you should check out. Keep in mind that although there's plenty of girl-on-girl porn out there, almost all straight porn has girls getting it on with girls, too. Also, if you do go the girl-on-girl route, you can either get stuff directed by men for men that tends to have more boobacious, longer-fingernailed straight chicks in it, or you can get stuff directed by and starring lesbians. The excellent thing about the lesbo stuff is that it actually shows real, hot sex between women who love fucking women. The not-excellent thing about the lesbo stuff is some straight girls might be turned off by the butchiness of it all. Plenty of lesbian porn features femme actresses, but a lot of it also has more masculine-looking women, and some straight girls can't handle that. It all depends on what you want.

Once you get a taste of what's out there, pay attention to which production companies you like, which directors are good, and which porn stars turn you on, and the porn forest will suddenly be easier to thrash your way through.

Porn Note: If you rent a DVD instead of a VHS, you may be given the option of seeing stuff from alternate angles. Can't quite see the tongue on that clit? Hard to tell how deep that finger's gone up her pussy? Take a look at it again from a different P.O.V.

The thing I find so important about stuff like porn, sex shops, clubs, books, websites, toys, and workshops is that they, unlike mass society, embrace the multitude of ways that people experience sexual pleasure. They give those who might otherwise feel like loner freaks a nod of approval that says "You're fine, you're with us." I hate to think of some poor soul who loves licking feet wandering around hating himself, thinking there's something seriously wrong with him. Luckily, there are plenty of clubs and websites dedicated to foot fetishes where someone like that could feel at home. I even saw a pair of rubber feet for sale in a sex shop, thank you very much.

There is nothing wrong with any sexual act as long as everyone involved is having fun. There are so many ways you can feel like shit about yourself; having a healthy sexual imagination just shouldn't be one of them. We're on this earth once and for such a short time that spending life repressed and freaked out is a waste. Especially when there's so much fun to be had! What's the point of being here if not to experience it?

chapter seven

And Boy Makes Three!

A good three-way is like jumping out of a plane. It's not how I want to travel all the time, but it's thrilling, kind of reckless, and something I think back on with a grin.

—BONNIE, 46

*F*or a lot of ladies, getting it on with a guy and a girl at the same time is the icing on the bi-curious cake. Not only do you get to experience different parts of your sexuality at the same time, but you get to do it in a naughty and taboo situation. You get to play with both the hard and the soft, feasting on whatever it is about both of these that turns you on—it's like having dinner and dessert at the same time. Adding another body to the mix also increases your options—you can watch or be watched, eat or be eaten, fuck or be fucked, or all of it simultaneously in various configurations. A three-way can inspire you to push your boundaries and give you a whole new take on sex. As Marina, 39, describes it: "I'd been sleeping with her for a while and was already really attracted to her, but having a guy there who I was also hot for made it even better."

For some women, keeping a guy in the mix is essential for their enjoyment of same-sex experimentation. If you're in a committed relationship but still want to satisfy your bi-curiosity, for example, you may feel like you're cheating if he's not there. Or maybe you fear that it's too lesbian for comfort without a guy around. Then there are those women whose biggest turn-on comes from being watched by a guy, rather than from the sex with the other chick itself.

And as far as the male perspective goes, I think it's safe to say that almost every straight guy with a pulse is into the idea of two chicks getting it on. "I think because there's no man there, that it's pure female, pure lust, that's what gets us," says Richard, 31. Tony, 36, says, "Women's bodies are such a turn-on. Watching them play with each others' tits and eat each other out is fucking great! Especially if I get to join in."

If you are into the idea of a threesome, whether or not you're up for making it a reality is a different story. Just like with any fantasy, there's a big difference between what you think about to get off and what you really want to act on in your real life. Group sex can be a rockin' good time, but it can also be dangerous, especially if there are some serious feelings involved. If you're in a relationship, your partner might hear your suggestion of a third as "You're inadequate. I need some help here!" Also, what seems like a good time at first can end up as a very un-fun situation. Are you sure you can handle watching your lover get it on with someone else? And some guys may not be as turned on as they thought they'd be watching their girlfriends discover that they love eating pussy. I spoke to Marshall, 33, who was married to a woman who'd slept with a bunch of chicks before settling down with him:

I was threatened by her female experiences so I turned them into fantasy in order to try and remove the threat. In bed I'd have her talk about being with other women to get me off, and it eventually elevated to this point where I became kind of obsessed with it. She didn't really want to have a three-way but she encouraged me to try it so I could see that it wasn't the huge deal I was making it out to be. I'd built it up so much in my head as a fantasy but the reality ended up being completely different. It was a huge letdown. I ended up feeling jealous and left out. Watching someone you really care about have sex with another person is an experiment the human heart isn't prepared for.

Keep in mind that sex can bring up a lot of insecurities, and an ill-orchestrated three-way can be more hurtful than fun. It's not like one-on-one sex where all your attention is flowing in one direction and vice versa. When there are several people in the mix, the physical and emotional logistics are more challenging, and you have to take different things into consideration. This is why it's important to try and get your head in the right space and to go about this adventure in the right way with the right people.

Hooking up with a couple of people at the same time can happen organically and be no big deal, but sometimes it's not that simple and getting into it, or out of it, can be a little tricky. The following are some suggestions that I hope will help you get the most out of your three-way experience.

Wrapping Your Head Around It

I'll just go ahead and assume here that the majority of your sexual encounters involve you and just one other person. This means that a bit of mental shifting has to happen when you take on two partners at once. Even if you've had threesomes before, each time it happens you'll have to check in with yourself to see how you feel about the particular situation. You may find you have to tend to a little mental letting go before diving in.

Letting Go of Attachments

Whether you're getting it on with your partner, strangers, or friends, the more you're able to open your mind and free yourself from the possessiveness surrounding sex the better. There are some couples out there who bring in a third as an expression of their love and trust for each other, and some who have full-on relationships with more than one person at a time, but usually three-ways are more about fun and adventure. Not getting caught up in attachment and expectation can make or break the experience, especially for those of you who are bringing a third into an intimate relationship. This is not a time to take sex personally. This is a time to take sex as a physical act. Watching your girlfriend or boyfriend enjoying fucking someone else can be rough, but if you can see it as just sex, and enjoy the fact that someone you care about is receiving pleasure, then you'll have a lot more fun. Being clear about how you feel and communicating with your partner here is vital. Personally, I can't imagine having a threesome with someone I was in love with—it would make me miserable—but there are plenty of couples out there for whom it works.

I've only had threesomes with people I wasn't in love with, and every time I did it I had big fat fun. These situations require some letting go as well—you have to keep your ego and insecurities in check and remember that everyone is trying to negotiate a confusing physical situation with way more body parts than they're used to. Chances are very good that if you're not getting any attention it's because someone's too busy, not because you have fat thighs. It'll be more fun if you can remove yourself from your usual expectations about getting attention and instead enjoy the fact that you're in this wild situation where you get to watch someone other than yourself have sex for a change.

> I'm in a committed relationship with a man and one thing I think that's really important is that we don't hang around with the women we sleep with. We're not pals, it's a separate thing. It makes it easier to be no big deal.
>
> —ALICE, 39

Letting Go of Judgments

Another thing that may take you an extra moment to get your head around is the fact that you're not having "normal" sex, the kind that happens between two people. The fact that you're sleeping with another woman takes it that much further out of the ordinary. This kink factor can either get you off massively or stop you in your tracks. If you can't get over the feeling that you're doing something wrong or bad, you won't be able to let yourself go and have fun. Rather than focus on what your parents/coworkers/children might think, I suggest you turn your thoughts to how adventurous you're being. A major part of the thrill of having sex outside the box is that you're having sex outside the box. Make it a good thing rather than a bad one. Focus on things like the fact that you're being brave enough to act out a fantasy, that you're pushing the sexual envelope, and that you're allowing yourself to have a truly memorable experience. Get off on being a naughty girl, and you'll have much more fun.

> I love how secretly jealous my friends are when I tell them about my group sexcapades. They act shocked but they always want details.

—ELANA, 26

Letting Go of Fear

For some people, entering into a group sex situation brings up a lot of fears. Here are a couple of the most common concerns I came across.

1. What if everyone else knows what they're doing, and I don't? Now I'll look like an idiot in front of two people rather than just one!

As with any sort of sex, the more you let yourself feel it and go with the flow, the better a lover you'll be. Three-ways are a little more confusing than having sex with just one other person, but if you really notice what's going on around you, let yourself feel it and enjoy it, you can negotiate it no problem. The excellent bonus is that you can step out for a moment, pull up a chair and just watch the other two go at it. This can be a huge turn-on as well as a great way to notice what your partners are into; then you can jump back in and wow them with your new knowledge.

2. What if they're into each other more than they're into me?

This is something you can't really control; it's just a risk you have to take. You can increase your chances of not having your adventure turn out this way if you make sure you have great chemistry with at least one of the people you're sleeping with. Even if you're going at it with total strangers, you should be able to get some idea of how much lust there is between you before you climb into the sac (a hot make-out session beforehand is a good way to get the juices flowing). If you're doing it with people you know, make sure that they're considerate and thoughtful and will make you feel included. For those of you who can truly let go of your attachments you can see it as a great opportunity to sit back and watch two people get it on who are really hot for each other.

> It made me realize that women don't need men to have a good time in bed. It was very educational but intense.
>
> —ALAN, 26

vocabulary builder

SIDE DISH:
a person who hooks up with a couple
for a three-way

The Negotiations

Once you've wrapped your head around the idea you can get down to making your three-way happen. There are countless ways a couple of girls can wind up in bed with a boy—you and your boyfriend might invite in a female third, you and the chick you're sleeping with could bring in a guy, or you and a bunch of drunk strangers could meet at a party, bar, bus stop, wherever, and decide to get it on. Depending on the circumstances you'll either end up negotiating beforehand, or it'll happen more spontaneously. In the latter case, two people usually just start fooling around and the third joins in. If you find yourself in this situation and it feels right, go for it. But if you're in a relationship and haven't come to some sort of understanding beforehand, it's important to check in with your partner. Don't just assume that because you've found some hot chick, your boyfriend will automatically be into the idea of jumping in on whatever action you've started. Just because it's another chick doesn't mean it doesn't count—he may not be into sharing you with anyone.

If you're going to negotiate beforehand, figuring out how to broach the subject can be a little difficult. How touchy it will be depends on how much you have at stake, how comfortable you are talking about sex in general, and what your relationship is like. Telling someone you're having a relationship with that you want to sleep with somebody else is a pretty loaded thing to do. Here are a few things to keep in mind.

- Put yourself in their place. If the tables were turned, how would you want to hear that your partner was interested in a three-way? What would make you feel the most confident that it was about having fun, not that there was something lacking in your relationship?

- Have a talk about sex. Ask what your partner's always wanted to try and tell him or her what your wish list is. Suggesting a third in this context will put it in perspective as just another thing that turns you on rather than something threatening.

- Rent a porn movie that has two women and a guy doing it. Say something like "I've always wanted to try that. Does it do anything for you?" Make it playful and fun. If they take the bait, great; if not don't push it.

> Most girls are curious to begin with but never would have done it without prodding from their boyfriends.
>
> —CHRISTINA, 22

Warning: If you can tell your partner isn't into it, don't keep at them until they give in. If they do it against their will just to please you, they'll probably wind up super-resentful and jealous. Likewise, you shouldn't participate in anything you don't want to just to please someone else. These situations can be tough to navigate emotionally even when you're game; if you're not into it, I can't imagine it being anything but awful. In these cases it's better to just relegate three-ways to the fantasy world.

> Bringing another woman into our bed made our relationship stronger. We found out how much we trust each other on a whole new level.
>
> —EVAN, 33

Negotiating with a Friend

Friends are great to sleep with because you get the trust-and-caring part without having to commit to anything. Friends are not great to sleep with because you lose the trust-and-caring part if things get weird. Even mentioning that you want to have sex with a friend can create a wedge, so the idea of a three-way should be handled with some delicacy. I recommend bringing it up as casually as possible. Get into a conversation about sex; tell them what's going on with the guy or girl you're sleeping with and mention you're looking for a third. If the reaction is anything but horrified, move on to the next step: "Wanna join us?" (It's a good idea to broach the subject with your friend when it's just the two of you. Bringing along your lover could put your friend on the spot and create a more awkward situation. The less people involved, the less pressure.) Keep it fun and light and see where it goes.

Negotiating with a Stranger

In this situation, the only thing at stake is your pride. You can be more brazen because you have less to lose, plus you've got a partner in crime to help you out. Depending on how good a flirt you are, going out to find your unknown third can be a lot of fun.

- Go to a bar or a club with your lover and look around for someone you both think is hot. Send the person a drink and tell the bartender to say it's from both of you. If you're holding hands and looking seductively their way, they should get the point.

- Go up to a hottie and strike up a conversation. Tell them, "My boyfriend [or girlfriend] thinks you're hot," and then point across the room to where your partner stands looking on.

🍒 If you're two girls looking for a male third, start making out in some public, straight-guy kind of place. When you come up for air, survey your fan club, find the cutest one, and wave him over.

🍒 If you're out with a guy and looking for a female third, have him flirt with her first and make a connection before you come up and join them. When you do, make it clear you're together (give him a big kiss or hold his hand) and then shake her hand, smiling, maybe saying something suave like "My boyfriend has excellent taste." This is a good way to pick up straight girls who are open to the surprise chick bonus.

🍒 If you're out and you see a hot third (or you're alone and you see a hot couple), hold up three fingers and give them a sly smile. This happened to me at a bar once—the guy discreetly put three fingers on his upper arm while he winked at us over his shoulder. Super cheesy, but sometimes it's easier to be cheesier.

What's not to like? You're either having two hotties work you at the same time or you're sitting back and watching them get it on.

—Tom, 48

Finding Your Group

Finding someone to round out your three-way is much the same as finding someone to go on a regular old date with, although some places are more conducive than others to group sex. You can definitely hook up in all the standard places—at parties, concerts, and bars; through friends; on-line—but I highly recommend keeping an eye out for hotels or parties where there are hot tubs, cheesy as it sounds. Climbing into small pools of hot water with scantily clad, tipsy people is likely to get you where you want to go faster than hanging out at your best friend's wedding. Strip clubs are good, too, since there's a built-in naughtiness to them and people already have sex on the brain. And I'd have to add that anywhere where there's tons of booze is pretty much always a good bet. An uncanny number of group sex tales begin "So one time me and my friends were really wasted and . . ."

Working with All Those Body Parts

Once you find all the players, it's time to let the games begin. Having sex with more than one person at the same time is incredibly exciting, but it can be overwhelming, too. Before we get down to logistics there are a few basic Three-Way Rules you should be aware of:

Rule #1: Check in every once in a while to make sure everyone's being taken care of. Sometimes people like to sit back and watch, which is fine, but if it seems like someone's just lying there waiting for attention, expand your grope to include them.

Rule #2: Nobody has to do anything they don't want to do, no matter how into it the other two are. If you don't want to play, just sit out a round and watch them go at it without you. And don't you pressure anybody else, either.

Rule #3: Pay attention. There's going to be a lot of input coming from all directions, and the more tuned in and open you are, the more fun everyone will have. For example, if you're lying on your stomach eating her out and he's trying to swing your ass around so he can schtupp you, don't be so into your munching that you don't budge. Be aware that something else is going on at the same time and go with the flow.

Rule #4: Share. Don't get greedy and take all the goodies for yourself. Get into it, absolutely, but don't hog his hard-on the whole time or keep your face buried in her crotch where no one else can have any. There's plenty to go around, so nobody should be going hungry.

Rule #5: Don't forget to sit back and watch. One of the big bonuses of three-ways is you get an eyeful as well as a pantful of fun. If you get off watching people have sex, here's your chance to see it live in person.

Strike a Pose

Taking on two people at once can be clumsy, but it's not rocket science. If you pay attention, talk to each other, and just do what feels good, you're bound to have a good time. Here are some fun poses you might want to wind up in:

Positions

- Lay him on his back with one girl sitting on his face while the other rides his cock. The girls can play with each other's tits and make out while they do this. A variation on this pose is to have a girl lying on her back with the other girl sitting on her face while the guy fucks the first girl.
- Both girls hump each other in the missionary position while he crawls on top and fucks the girl on the top from behind and fingers the one on the bottom.
- Have one girl lie on her back while the other kneels on top of her, fingering and humping her pussy. Have him kneel and straddle the girl on the bottom so the girl on top can suck him off. This puts the girl

on the bottom in a great spot to finger his butthole or spank his ass.

🍒 One girl stands with her legs spread and her body leaning over the bed. He stands on the floor and fucks her from behind while she eats out the other girl, who is lying on her back on the bed.

🍒 Have him lie on his back while one girl lies on her stomach on each side of him. Both girls blow him at the same time, alternately making out and sucking his cock while he fingers one girl with his left hand and the other with his right.

🍒 Sit him in a chair and tie his hands behind his back so he can't jerk off. Let him watch while you and the other girl put on a show. Every once in a while give him a teeny bit—lick his cock or stick it in you for just a second—and then get back on the bed. Play around with her until he can't take it anymore, and then release him and let him have at both of you.

Get creative and just follow what feels right. You can elaborate on any position by bringing in dildos, vibrators, blindfolds, whatever. You can order each other around, role-play, or take it into the shower. The following are some real-life scenarios to help get your imagination flowing:

My first bisexual experience happened by a game of truth or dare. I ended up making out with my friend while our husbands watched. From there it went to her daring me to eat her pussy. We were pretty drunk by that time and just started going at it. We wouldn't let the men participate but they jerked off while they watched us which made it even hotter.

–Julie, 23

The two times my boyfriend and I have been with another woman it was never planned, it just happened organically. One time I was at a party and this woman was being really flirty with me. My boyfriend was right there, so she knew I was with him, but it didn't seem to bother her so I went along with it. I kind of pushed to see how far she'd go, if she was serious. I'd drop hints like, "I wonder what's in that room, have you been back there?" and she took the bait. We found a room that wasn't being used and the three of us locked ourselves in there. The sex was mostly her and me and him and me, there was a little between them but he was mostly just with me. There was no weirdness between me and my boyfriend afterward, because we're really strong together. This isn't something we go out and do all the time, but the time was just right so we went for it.

–Tory, 49

I worked with this girl who I had crazy sexual tension with. We went out one night after work and had a drink at a hotel bar. This very attractive lady came up and started chatting us up. She flirted heavily with both of us and finally invited us up to her room. When we got up there the two of them sat on one bed and I sat on the other and the lady opened a bottle of wine. Before they'd had even a sip the lady leaned over and started making out with my friend. I watched for a while before jumping in myself. Before long, I was eating out the lady while my friend sucked me off. It was a good time.

–Bob, 46

I was hanging out at a friend's house one night and she suggested that we start making out. I'd fooled around with her before so it was no big deal except that this time her boyfriend was there. We took off our shirts and started kissing and she said, "You have really nice tits," and she started sucking them and then her boyfriend came over and started sucking them too.

We decided to take a shower and she went down on me right away. She's straight, but she went for it like a pro. And I was kissing her boyfriend while she ate me out. It was so fun because I trusted him and she's so hot. We all got out and got into bed and she asked me to sit on her face so I did. And then her boyfriend ate her out while she ate me out. When I got off her she asked if she was any good at eating my pussy and I said, "Let me show you." So I started eating her out while her boyfriend made out with her. He was playing with her tits while I fucked her with my fingers and ate her out. It was so hot.

—Amy, 34

I have this friend who's always getting into these crazy sex situations. I told her the next time something goes down to give me a call, so one night she calls and tells me she's hanging out with this hot chick and they want me to come over and fuck them. So I go over and they sit me down in the living room and we just hang out for a while. I was kind of nervous because they had this whole thing going on and knew each other really well, but I knew it was going to be hot so I got over it. I went into the bathroom and when I came out they were sitting on the bed waiting for me. I sat down and started making out with one of them while she fingered the other girl. Pretty soon thereafter all our clothes came flying off.

−Patrick, 38

While on your quest to acquire stories of your own, perhaps a little game is just what you need to liven up your party of three. One of my favorites is the Ten Commandments, and it goes like this: Write down the following commands on ten pieces of paper, stick them in a hat or a drawer near the bed, and take turns pulling them out and following the instructions.

The Ten Commandments

Sit in a chair by the bed and boss the other two around. You can only watch and touch yourself (they can't touch you).	Tie one of your bedmates to the bed by his or her wrists and perform oral sex on them while the third party fucks you, or gives you oral, from behind
Give hand jobs to the other two parties while they perform oral on you at the same time.	Everybody lie on their sides and perform oral sex on each other, going in a circle to your right.
Rub baby oil all over the tits of the other girl. Lie on top of her and hump her while the guy fingers you both from behind.	Have the other two blindfold you and kiss you all over your body, everywhere but your genitals. Have them whisper filthy things in your ears and when you can take it no more, tell them how you want them to get you off.
You are the slave and the other two are your masters. Do whatever they tell you to.	Get on all fours and eat one person out while the other does you from behind.
Sit the person of your choice in a chair, tie their hands behind their back, and then you and the other person show off for them. Be as sexy and wild as you can, get them as crazed with desire as possible and then blow/eat them out in the chair, still tied up, until they come.	Tie one person to the chair and the other to the bed. Fuck around with one while the other watches, but don't let either one come; stop just before and switch to the other person. When you feel you've tortured them enough, untie them and all of you go at it together.

I don't know if any of this three-wayness sounds appealing or whether all those limbs and genitals flying around just make you dizzy, but if you're game for it and you find yourself a good situation, there's really nothing like it. Just make sure you're emotionally prepared, safe, and communicating with your partners and you'll have a great time.

chapter eight

Pussywhipped,
or Going Back to Boyville?

> I love my girlfriend, we have a great thing going, I don't really think about being straight. All that matters to me is that I'm in a good relationship.
>
> —MARYANNE, 24

ow that you've woken up this other side of yourself—how big a part of you is it? Could you see going back for more, or was sex with a girl just something you needed to try out? Did you wind up in a relationship or was it just another roll in the hay? And for those of you who've only experienced another woman with a guy involved, are you up for a little one-on-one? There are a lot of factors that can determine where you go from here. Depending on where you are in your life, your current relationship status, how comfortable you are with your sexuality, and how much you liked or disliked the experience, you can either go back to the boys, stick with the girls, or do both in varying degrees.

After experimenting with women a part of me just decided to close that door; it just seemed too confusing.
—Kelly, 32

When making your decision, figuring out what it all means in terms of your sexuality can be the hardest part to grapple with. Many of you who've considered yourselves straight your whole lives never gave your sexualities a second thought, and now that you've crossed the line some questions might suddenly be popping up that aren't so easy to answer. What does it mean that you can connect and have hot sex with a woman? If you wind up in a relationship with a chick, what does that mean? Can you be attracted to both men and women yet still really only want to "be" with men? Are you straight, bisexual, or lesbian? And what the hell does any of that mean?

As I mentioned in the intro, sexuality is a ginormous, squirrely topic—you could spend a lifetime reading up on it and arguing about it, and, as far as I'm concerned, in the end you'd pretty much just have to decide for yourself what it all means. Because all the definitions of bi, straight, gay, lesbian I've come across seem to be as mercurial as human nature itself. I gleaned what I could from my own research and experiences as well as through those of my friends, and I discovered that while one source's definition of "straight" didn't involve the possibility of sleeping with the same sex, another source's did. I learned that while some people define themselves as bisexual, many people look down upon the term as indecisive, as a phase you pass through on your way to being gay, or as a cop-out used by homosexuals who want to reap the benefits of being semi-heterosexual. It seemed every definition of every sexuality had major discrepancies, and as if anyone attempting to adhere to certain rules would wind up failing sooner or later. Volumes have been written on the topic, and careers have been spent dissecting it, but as far as I can tell defining sexuality is a never-ending work in progress. So I say, just use whatever definition works for you—assuming you care to define yourself at all, that is.

One theory that has really worked for me puts sexual behaviors on a spectrum, with total straighties on one end and total gays on the other. Developed by Dr. Alfred Kinsey in the late 1940s, the Kinsey Scale rates sexual behavior on a 6-point continuum, with 0 being exclusively heterosexual, 6 being exclusively homosexual, and 3 being equal parts of both. Kinsey 1 and 2 are mostly heterosexual with homosexual tendencies, while 4 and 5 are mostly homosexual with heterosexual tendencies. Factors like fantasies, dreams, sexual activities, and romantic attachments figure into where you rate, and you can move around on the spectrum as you discover new things about yourself. I like this model for its vagueness. It's not meant to be used as a way to define your sexuality, so it doesn't offer labels to go along with its numerical values but instead gives perspective as to where you fit into the vast sea of sexual possibilities. This is helpful when you stray from the absolutes of 0 and 6 into the more murky territory in between because you don't have to adhere to any rules. It eliminates the possibility of failure that comes with labeling and lets you find your place in a more liberal system of classification.

> I never considered myself a lesbian, but that's not to say that I wasn't committed to my ex-girlfriend. When I fell for my boyfriend I remember thinking to myself, *I am so getting off on his maleness.* I remember thinking the same thing with my ex-girlfriend. *I'm so getting off on her femaleness.* Maybe that's what a bisexual is. It isn't a burning issue for me, though, I'm not interested in getting it defined, and not interested in being defined by it either.
>
> —ROBYN, 37

So what's the big whoop about defining sexuality and classifying yourself as one thing or another, anyway? If you can enjoy whatever situation you're in without picking it apart or being bothered by people with inquiring minds, then there is no big whoop. As far as I'm concerned it only matters if it helps you figure out who you are and what it is you need to be happy. And even then it doesn't have to mean putting a label on your sexuality, exactly, but more just figuring out who (if anyone) you're into being with. If you know you eventually want to be in a committed relationship with a man but enjoy messing around with women, for example, you need to be honest with yourself and the chicks you're sleeping with. Sleeping with girls may just be flingy and fun, but if you wind up having an emotional connection with someone it can get very confusing, which can hurt you or her or both of you. The clearer you are about what you want, the easier it'll be to remain grounded.

I know this because my innocent dabble turned into dating a woman and it threw me for a serious loopdy-loo. The thought of being in a relationship with a chick had never before crossed my mind. My previous dabblings were quick and fun and I'd always just assumed I was straight, but when I got with her and stayed with her for a while, I suddenly felt like I had to figure some things out.

It just didn't make sense to me that we could have so much fun, have such great sex, and connect on such a deep level and not live happily ever after. So I picked at it from all angles. I tried to figure out where love and attraction come from and what they really mean. I wondered about my attachment to being straight and where it comes from. If we were raised in a lesbian society, and all those women who wanted to lead heterosexual lives had to come out and go against the flow, would the majority of us be with women instead? Would I? Was I succumbing to my straight-world conditioning when in reality I could be with either men or women?

In hindsight, I'd say I'm about a 1 ½ on the Kinsey scale, but for some reason I was putting all this pressure on myself to be a 6 or at the very least a 3. Like I was being dishonest with both of us unless I could cough up a few more homo points, when in reality I should have just been in it, had fun, and kept in closer touch with the way I felt. I ended up confusing the hell out of myself and torturing her and all my friends by waffling over our relationship: "I want this"; "I want this not." I swirled around and around until I finally just had to admit to myself that I wasn't feeling it. As unsophisticated as this explanation is, it's the best I can do. There were specific things about us as two people together that made the relationship not work, obviously, but the end also had to do with the fact that she was a woman. As hard as I tried and as much as I loved her, I couldn't take what was going on seriously as a romantic relationship. I couldn't get past the feeling that I was playing, having this outrageously hot and fun time with one of my best friends rather than a serious love relationship. This is not to say that all my relationships with men have made perfect sense, but at least they've made more sense to me in my gut as something I really want (albeit in different circumstances with different people most of the time!). With my girlfriend it was hard for me to discern where my feelings were coming from—my gut, or my conditioning. It still is, to a certain degree.

> My friends were asking me if I had been gay my whole life and if I was coming out now. At the time, I wasn't sure. I could relate to my girlfriend on many levels as a woman, but I couldn't as a gay woman. I hadn't dealt with the issues, hadn't fought for my rights, I didn't feel part of the politics. I was with a woman and I wasn't sure I could be for the long haul. In the end there was a point where I felt myself choosing and I was choosing no.
>
> —CARRIE, 41

The truth is it's not so easy to know what you want if you've never experienced it before. Regardless of whether you're having a fling with a stranger or a romantic evening with someone you adore, you could discover things about yourself that you didn't know before. You could get totally caught up in the excitement of it all and think you're in love when you're really not. Or you could actually fall in love with a woman even though you were just in it for fun. Or sex with women could be something that you always wanted to try, that you fantasized and dreamed about forever, but that you ended up not liking at all once you took the plunge, no matter how many different women you tried sleeping with. There are plenty of ways it can go, and often you really can't know until you try. All you can do is keep an open mind and as firm a grip on who you really are as possible.

As with any relationship with anyone, a bazillion factors go into how it turns out, and what the relationship looks like is ultimately up to those involved. But it's still interesting looking at things through a broad lens to see how your own experiences match up.

Flinging

Some women never get into anything serious with other chicks; they just gobble up some hot sex every now and then and head back to the boys. I'm not great at one-night stands with guys, and I'm not all that into it with women, either; for me, there usually has to be some sort of connection for the sex to be any good. But I talked to plenty of ladies that could care less about that. Or who fucked good friends, whom they did have connections with, and just continued on with the friendship with zero weirdness. "Me and certain friends just hook up sometimes. We're usually wasted," said Melanie, 20. "I wouldn't want to date any of them or anything. We're all straight. It's just a fun thing we do sometimes."

Many women have flings with chicks not only because they like the sex, but because they feel it frees them from the male world and lets them be more in control of the sexual terrain. It's as if they feel more empowered because they don't have to deal with male objectification—they can have a fun and sexy time on more equal terms with someone. This is absolutely true, yet there's another side to the coin that I think we all need to be aware of. We as a culture have been trained to view women as sex objects, and even in sexual situations between women, the male-inspired objectification of our sex can still seep in. This is because the straight world constantly bombards us with images of women as sex objects and nothing more, and even if we find it repulsive, it's what we're used to seeing. It's so deeply imbedded in our subconscious that even if we think we're being all sexy and liberated by getting it on with other chicks, we may just be mimicking the bad male habits we're so used to.

There's nothing wrong with one-night stands or mutual objectification between lovers—and yes, women do it to men all the time, too—but the last thing we need is for our sisters to be out there perpetuating the notion that we're just a bunch of hot things to fuck. I'm not saying you shouldn't have one-night stands, nor am I saying that you should never objectify another woman (because I think that can be hot), but I am saying that you're capable of doing some damage without realizing it. No matter how thrilling and sexy your adventures are, still treat everyone with respect and enter into this with your eyes open.

Relationshipping

There's also the possibility that your experience will go beyond flinging and get more serious. Just because you consider yourself straight doesn't mean you can't fall ass over teacups for some girl and wind up in a relationship. "She was the only woman I've ever been with, but I was really in love with her," says Charlotte, 38, "I don't know if I'll ever have another girlfriend—I'm not usually attracted to women—but I'm not ruling it out."

Having a girlfriend can be such a great thing. Many women love it for how nurturing it is and how much easier it is to process "issues" because you're both coming at them from the same direction. "It's like you get your lover and your best friend all wrapped up in one," said Margie, 47. Some women loved not having to seek male approval and others loved how hot it felt to break the rules.

Even if you feel all of these things, you might find it a little freaky and disorienting to be with a woman in the kind of intense relationship you usually reserve for men. As I mentioned earlier, just try to stay in touch with how you feel and go with the flow. It can be a lot to wrap your head around, but if you've found someone you have big fat feelings for and who makes you really happy, why not just go with it? All the women I spoke with who were unconcerned with what being in the relationship meant were the ones who were able to enjoy it the most. They were able to live in the moment and just be happy that they'd found someone they loved being with. Those of us who tortured ourselves and demanded an explanation had a lot less fun.

One alarming thing I noticed, which everyone should keep in check, is that a lot of women who get with a chick for the first time get all cranky at men. I heard a lot of "I've never been treated this well by a guy"; "The sex is so hot—women just know how to touch you better than a guy does"; "You just have this connection with women that you don't have with guys. You don't have to explain everything to someone who'll probably never understand anyway." And on and on and on.

This all may be true, but as with any new relationship, the novelty wears off and you suddenly notice, "Oh, yeah, this is a person complete with luggage and quirks and maybe they're not as perfect as I made them out to be." I just think the delusions of grandeur can be worse when we get with a woman because being with a woman is newer than being with any new guy. When you start dating a new guy, you run down the comparison list as to why he's so much better than the last one, but with the chick thing you don't just lambaste the old guy, you take down the entire male half of the species! We're so thrilled by the differences in communication and sex along with the fact that it's a whole new person that we go a little hog wild on the whole "Men suck" thing. It's like all our old relationships with men are being held up to this sparkly, shiny, as yet unscathed new one with a woman. A woman we haven't been with long enough to have any of her warts shine through. Not very fair at all. To anyone. It's not until the shine starts to fade that you settle into thinking "Hmmm, do I really want to be with this woman? Do I really want to be with a woman at all?" (Then you proceed to take down the entire female half of the population.) Just a cautionary note to those of you who are all gung ho on your fabulous new relationship with your girlfriend. Have a great time, but be realistic, too.

sleeping with chicks tip #5

Lesbians beware! After an uncommunicative
relationship with a man, straight chicks eat up
being spoiled by a woman. Then in about
six months they realize it's great
but they really want a man.

Playing Girl House

If you and your girlfriend wind up really getting along, maybe you'll want to think about moving in together. Shacking up with your girl can be such an exciting thing. It's like a permanent slumber party with your best friend, whom you also get to have hot sex with. There are obviously plenty of things that living with your girlfriend has in common with living with your boyfriend, like arguing over housework, decorating together, and figuring out whose furniture is better, but there are definitely some things that are very living-with-your-girlfriend specific. The whole U-Haul thing for example. Chicks move in together so fast it's ridiculous—the old joke "What does a lesbian bring on her second date?" "A U-Haul" exists for a *vocabulary builder*

L.B.D. (LESBIAN BED DEATH)
When two women are having a sexual
relationship and the friendship aspect
overpowers the sex aspect
and stifles it completely.

reason. What's up with that? "It escalates real quickly and gets intense quickly because women give a lot more with their hearts right away," says Sandra, 44. "Since I was used to men being more aloof, it was like gluttony. I ate it up and dove in." If you do decide to live with your girlfriend, here are a few of the pros and cons you may share with some of the women I spoke with:

Love It

- I like having a house full of female energy. It's not necessarily better than living with a guy, just noticeably different. There's something more nurturing about it whereas with guys it feels more stark and practical or something.

- It's easier to get in synch menstrual-wise which makes sex a lot easier.
- If you're the same size, your wardrobe doubles.
- When your body is in a knot and you're moaning from period cramps she can empathize with how you feel. It really helps having someone just feel your pain sometimes.
- It's like a secret club, no boys allowed! It touches on something magical and sacred for me.
- You get to share all your facial and hair products. I've never been with a guy who brings anything even remotely decent in that department to the table.
- Coming home after a hard day and getting all your problems off your chest can be much more satisfying with a woman. Men usually try to fix the problems. Women can just listen.
- All your sex toys are in the same building. You don't suddenly realize in the middle of sex that you left the strap-on that fits you better at your house with your favorite glittery vibrator. This totally rules.

Hate It

- If you live with your girlfriend but still call yourself straight, people get up your ass even more than they do if you're just dating.

- Women get so involved in each other's lives that they get codependent and it feels like you can't breathe.

- There's a built-in empathy that women have for each other that's great in many ways but can also be really negative. It can lead to LBD. For example, and this may sound bad, but in a straight relationship, most guys will put a little more pressure on you to have sex if you're being lazy about it. A girl will understand and just give you a cuddle. A few too many nights like that and you're living with your best friend, not a girlfriend.

- You can never escape the endless overanalyzing! I can only talk about a relationship so much. Women are unstoppable. Is this what I put guys through?

- You have twice as much PMS to deal with. This is by far the most frightening part. I'm scared of myself when I have it, and I'm definitely scared of her when she does.

I think moving in with anyone is exciting—at first, anyway. It's this giant leap of faith that's sort of crazy and exciting and that takes sharing your life with someone to a whole new level. And if the situation turns out to be harmonious, it can be incredibly satisfying and comforting. Yet no matter how la-di-da your situation is, there will be some issues, and when it comes to living with your girlfriend, one issue that's rather large is the one of coming out.

Hello, World! Meet My Girlfriend!

Even if you still feel very attached to the straight world, if you're dating a woman you're going to have to decide how public you want to go with it. Coming out as a lesbian can be a huge fatty deal. Coming out as hetero-experimental probably won't be nearly as large, depending on how uptight the people around you are and how into the whole situation you are. It's not really making that loud of a statement or a commitment—telling people you sleep with chicks is like saying, "Hmmmm, I'm in the mood for spaghetti," while coming out as a lesbian is like saying, "I'm moving to Italy!"

Regardless of how intense your relationship is, you still have to decide how comfortable you are acting like a couple in public. Do you hold hands walking down the street? Will you plant one on her at a lesbian club but not at the local bar? Are you all hunky-dory in your apartment but not up for bringing a chick to a wedding or a work function? Carrie, 41, said, "I had trouble being public about it. And I knew how hurtful that was to her. We'd sometimes hold hands but I couldn't be that affectionate in public. I think because it went so far so quickly I didn't really have time to process what I was doing." Other women I spoke to had no problem at all; some even enjoyed upsetting the status quo by doing what they weren't supposed to do. And Susan, 20, said, "I felt a little weird being with a girl, I never wanted to come across as another sex symbol. People put women in all kinds of boxes and there's something about two women together in public that makes you feel like you're on display. There's such a 'thing' about it these days, you get way too much attention, like it's for them more than you."

You'll be dealing with feelings you haven't had before and it may take you a while to warm up to the idea of being seen in a different way. But if you're too freaked out to own up in public to the fact that you're with a chick, that sends your girl a yicky message, even if it's more about her womanness than her. Be sensitive to how gross it feels to be on the receiving end of that. She might be bothered by it, she might feel the same way you do, or she may understand that your brain is doing a tap-dance over the whole thing and give you time to figure it out. As always, the best thing to do is have a conversation about it and go from there.

Telling the Family

Your friends will probably just be intrigued; the people who will most likely perform the biggest freakout are your relatives. Even if they just love all your gay friends, the possibility of a "sexual deviant" right there in one's own family can make things a little squirrely. "I don't tell my family shit about any of the guys I date; I don't see why I'd tell 'em about a woman," said Cathy, 34. When I told my mom, she wasn't very surprised, but she wasn't exactly thrilled, either. I got the sense she felt like I was doing it just to piss her off—at first, anyway. Once it became clear that the relationship wasn't just a fling, she warmed up.

How you deal with your family depends on how open you are with them in general and how invested you are in your relationship with your girl. "I didn't tell my family—why bother? I'm just having fun," said Linda, 34. If you have the kind of relationship with your family where you tell them everything, then go ahead and give it a shot. But if you're more selective about what you share, and you know this would be upsetting, I say why bother, unless you're in a committed relationship. In that case, treat coming out as you would any delicate bit of news. Regardless of how happy and excited you are, it's a big deal to some people, and it's a lot for some parents to swallow. Don't be disappointed if they aren't jumping for joy at first. Give them time to get used to the fact. Let them in on your feelings about it and how hard/fun it is for you. Invite them over to meet your woman and show them how happy you are. It all depends on your relationship with them and how important it is to you that they know.

For the most part, the women I spoke with kept their relationships to themselves, but the ones who shared the information with their families got varied reactions.

> *I've sort of waffled back and forth between women and men my whole life. My dad was like, "I just got used to the idea of you being with a man and now you're with a woman again?" He found it confusing, but he was supportive.*
>
> —Francine, 38

> *My sister wanted to know everything—she was really*

curious, but married, and living vicariously through me. She was really excited for me.

—Sarah, 26

My parents wanted to know if this meant I was gay. The fact that I don't necessarily think I am made no sense to them, but I could tell they were relieved. Still, they really don't like to talk about it.

—Rachel, 31

My whole family thought it was no big deal. My parents are hippies and my mom had an affair with a woman a while back. Actually, so did my sister! The hardest one to tell was Dad, but he met my girlfriend and loved her, so it was fine.

—Holly, 22

vocabulary builder

HASBIAN:
an ex-lesbian

Even though it's nobody's business who you choose to partner up with, people definitely feel entitled to their opinions, and will most likely feel compelled to tell you about them if you're with another woman. Keep in mind that it's not your job to explain yourself to people who are having trouble with your choices. And if anyone gives you grief, just remember what Eleanor Roosevelt said (adapted to fit my point): "Nobody can make you feel like shit without your permission."

sleeping with chicks tip #6

If you're torn between whether you want to date a man or a woman next, you just have to decide whether you want dumb or crazy.

Over and Out

If you discover after your girl-on-girl escapade that what you really want is a good man, I highly doubt any of this will have been wasted time. Hardly anybody I talked to had regrets, and almost everybody was very grateful for her experiences. Heading back to Boyville was generally easy and most of the women made the transition with elevated self-confidence and newfound insights. Many found that being intimate with women allowed them to see more clearly how men work, as well as gave them a better understanding of what men go through being with them.

> Men have a tendency not to dwell on things—they tend to move forward, which drives me crazy sometimes but which I also really like. I feel like if I was with a woman I'd never get over stuff, we'd process our issues forever. I like the balance of being with a man.
>
> —KELLY, 32

Being with a woman really made me scrutinize what I'm attracted to and why. I had to admit that I was often attracted to guys who were unavailable, obsessive, or any number of other things that fed into my neuroses or my need to keep one foot out the door. Because we started out as good friends and had such a solid layer of trust and respect before we started sleeping together, I knew I was attracted to the woman I was with for all her excellent points. I think that's exactly why I tortured myself so much for not falling in love with her. I now realize that while there were great and true reasons to be in love, I just wasn't. And that's that. But I still feel it was an invaluable experience, that she was supportive and inspiring and left me feeling I'd raised the bar much higher for future relationships.

The women I spoke with had countless other revelations as a result of their experiences, some of which I'll get to later, but there were also some women who ended up having a pretty stinky time. Missy, 29, said, "I went for it because she was hitting on me so hard and I figured what the hell. I wasn't really into it and it left me feeling kind of yicky afterward." I don't think this is chick specific—sleeping with anyone you're not into sleeping with is going to make you feel gross. Similar reactions were had by other women who confessed they slept with a girl just to be cool or because their boyfriend or husband pressured them to. Again, doing something because you feel pressure to rather than because you genuinely want to usually results in disaster. And plenty of resentment! This is not to say these women would enjoy sleeping with chicks if it happened under healthier circumstances, but at least it wouldn't be doomed to fail from the get go.

> Women who've slept with other women seem more free sexually. And you can share tips about women with them, which is fun. It's a little scary, because you're always thinking in the back of your mind that they may leave you for a woman down the road.

—JEFF, 32

Some women also had worries regarding their heterosexuality and how it would now be perceived by men. Or just generally felt a little wobbly heading back to boyville. The following were some of the topics that came up the most:

Common Concerns About Returning to Boyville

1. *Now that I've tasted the fruits of the other side, how will I ever be satisfied with just having a man?* This was the most common concern, and one that I must confess I've thought about. It's like making a commitment just became that much harder—before, it was just about not fooling around with other men, now it's about not fooling around with the entire world! As much as my inner whore is crying about this one, I have to confess it only makes sense on a truly bratty level. You have to make sacrifices to be in a committed relationship with anyone, and if you're looking

for ways to make the grass greener on the other side you have plenty of options, regardless of whether you've slept both with sexes or not. Rather than looking at settling down with one person as missing out on revisiting sex with women, look at how lucky you were to have had the experience in the first place. I'd rather know how hot it is, and know it wasn't going to happen again, than not know, and regret that I never tried it.

2. *Will the men I'm with see other women as a threat?* Some women felt men would be wary of them, and that they could no longer embark on an innocent girls' night out without him wigging out. If you're with a guy like this, I imagine he wouldn't be able to trust you around other straight men, either, and in order for him to be comfortable, you'd have to hang out with just him, or him and a bunch of gay men, for the rest of your time together.

If you find yourself in this situation, you've either hooked up with a paranoid freak or you're not making a big enough effort to earn his trust and communicate with him. We all have plenty of things to feel insecure about in a relationship, and how much power that has over us depends on our ability to accept ourselves as well as our trust in our partners. If he's being jealous for no reason, that is a drag, and you should dump him. But if you're not making him feel secure that you're not going to stray, get off your ass and do something about it.

3. *Will men be turned on by my experiences and pressure me to have three-ways?* I can't imagine that any guy who finds you hot wouldn't be turned on by the thought of you with another woman, but whether he pressures you to sleep with one is another story. If he's really gung-ho and you're really not, there are plenty of ways to incorporate women into your fantasy life. You can talk dirty to him and tell him all the things you want to do to another woman while you're getting it on. You can masturbate in front of him and act like what you're doing to yourself is being done to you by another woman. You can put him in a dress and call him Shirley while he goes down on you. Or you can tell him it makes you uncomfortable and he needs to get over it.

I think the pros of sexual experimentation far outweigh most of the cons, because of my own experiences and those of the women I spoke with. If sleeping with a woman is something you want to try, I really hope you get to do it. And I hope it doesn't suck, because a positive, hot experience with a chick can give you invaluable things that being with a man can't. I'd like to leave off with some of the ways the women I spoke with felt forever changed by their experiences. Maybe they'll inspire you to get out there and get some stories of your own.

What I Learned at the All-Girl School:

It's made me more sensitive to men and more up-front about who I am with men. I'm less shy and I know exactly what I want in a relationship, so I won't put my energy into something where I won't get anything back.

I feel like I'm in more control of my sexuality. I'm straight, but I don't always need a man to turn me on. I feel empowered by this. Like I have some secret knowledge . . . It's hard to explain but I think it's made me more confident in my sexual encounters with men, better able to ask for and get what I want.

Being with an extraordinary woman was a real wake-up call to me about choosing better men. I realized that there are people who can be there more for me—that was very enlightening, and I will always be grateful.

It was very empowering. It made me feel like I didn't need men as much as I thought I did. Which improved my relationships with men, because the neediness went away.

One of the most amazing parts of being with another woman was realizing how incredibly soft and amazing women's bodies are. It was like falling into a cloud. It made me look at my own judgments about men's sexuality, how they walk around with their tongues hanging out, but after being with a woman I was like, "This is a fucking drug! No wonder men go crazy for it!"

I was able to tell my man how to go down on me better. And it's not because I was so good at it or anything, it's just that the chick I was with told me what to do. And when I got with a man afterwards and shared some of my new knowledge with him, the difference was incredible!

In a weird way, when I was with her I became the male in the sense that I found myself saying things like "I don't want to talk about this," "Why can't you take a simple yes or a no for an answer?" Etc. I started saying a lot of things men were always saying to me. I finally got what guys mean when they say women are too much. At times we can be so needy and want to overanalyze.

It made me better sexually with a man after being with a woman. I appreciated my body so much more afterwards. It was a really, really important thing. It teaches you so much about your body and how to love yourself more. I know a lot of women who could have benefited from it. It's been one of my greatest life experiences. I was very lucky with the timing and the person.

Troubleshooting

If you are experiencing problems while attempting to have sex with another woman, please use the following table to locate possible causes and solutions before contacting the author.

PROBLEM	POSSIBLE CAUSE	SOLUTION
Difficulty reading display.	You've never had sex with a woman before.	Ask her what she wants you to do to her.
Light comes on unexpectedly while engine is running.	Her significant other has returned home early from vacation.	Invite them to join in. Or run.
Makes strange noise when power's turned on.	She's hot for you.	Keep doing what you're doing.
Difficulty hooking up.	You're being too shy.	Tequila shots.

PROBLEM	POSSIBLE CAUSE	SOLUTION
Battery does not recharge.	Your curiosity has been satisfied. You're not into it.	Go back to sleeping with men.
Trouble turning on.	Nervousness, insecurity.	Tequila shots.
Nozzle control knob is jammed.	You're scared to eat pussy.	Reread Chapter 5.
Warning light comes on.	One of you is way more into it than the other.	Call it quits.
Smell on fingers won't fade.	Pussy perfume has a staying power rivaled only by garlic.	Enjoy all day long.
Menstrual cycles refuse to sync.	Not spending enough time together.	Exchange T-shirts and sniff the armpits three times a day.
Unit overheated.	You and your partner have excellent chemistry.	Continue to date.
Memory full.	You are cunt struck and can think of nothing else.	Stop pretending you're straight.
Communication error.	You're not used to dealing with women on this level of intimacy. You're used to guys who never want to talk.	Get a taste of your own medicine.

PROBLEM	POSSIBLE CAUSE	SOLUTION
Pause button doesn't respond.	Women don't have one.	Place her hand on her own crotch and whisper sweetly that you need to catch your breath.

appendix b

Resources

Books to Set the Mood

Affinity–Sarah Waters (Riverhead Books)

A brilliantly written and seductive novel about an inmate in a Victorian women's prison who has an affair with a lady visitor. Waters weaves a tale of suspense, lust, and mystery with her usual flair.

Beebo Brinker–Ann Bannon (Cleis Press)

The Queen of Lesbian Pulp Fiction, Ann Bannon, creates a vivid world of lust and suspense in her novel about an innocent butch woman who leaves Wisconsin for New York City and lands in the middle of the Beat-era lesbian scene.

Best Bisexual Women's Erotica–Cara Bruce, ed. (Cleis Press)

A collection of steamy stories ranging from the dark to the funny to the gender-bending. The book includes tales of women with women, women with men, women with both at the same time, and much more, providing the curious straight girl with plenty of things to sink her teeth into.

The Best of Lesbian Erotica–Tristan Taormino, ed. (Cleis Press)

A riveting group of stories about girl-on-girl sex ranging from the romantic to the perverse. Edited by a renowned sexologist and enthusiast.

Best S/M Erotica: Extreme Tales of Extreme Sex–M. Christian, ed. (Black Books)

An excellent erotic sojourn into the wide world of SM and fetish. It's got all sorts of stories about all sorts of gay, bi, and straight people doing all sorts of interesting things to each other in all sorts of exciting ways. It includes great tales of fantasy, role-playing, whips and handcuffs, and much more.

The Big Book of Lesbian Horse Stories–Alisa Surkis and Monica Nolan (Kensington)

A pulp fiction type collection of short, erotic stories with equestrian themes. This unique and very specific book contains stories about such things as lustful jockeys, curious farm girls, and dirty debutantes.

Cherry–Charlotte Cooper (Red Hot Diva)

A novel about a dyke running around London messing around with various chicks in an attempt to pop her lesbian cherry. Full of provocative sex scenes and down-and-dirty language.

Hot and Bothered 4: Short Short Fiction on Lesbian Desire–Karen Tulchinsky, ed. (Arsenal Pulp Press)

This book features 66 short stories of love and lust between women. Each story is 1,000 words or less, making it fun to read and a great source for those in need of a quick fix.

I Am My Lover: Women Pleasure Themselves–Joani Blank, ed. (Down There Press)

Beautiful photos of beautiful women of all ages gleefully getting themselves off. This book really blew my mind because not only are these women unashamed to masturbate, but they're brave enough to be photographed doing it! A must read for anyone who's intimidated about touching themselves. A very inspiring book.

Nice Girls Don't: Erotische Fotografien–Laurence Jaugey-Paget (Konkursbuchverlag)

A beautiful collection of color and black-and-white photographs taken of hot, butch babes in all sorts of compromising positions. I highly recommend this book to anyone who doesn't get the butch thing, because it's packed with shots and models that even the most skeptical will find sexy.

Nothing but the Girl–Susie Bright and Jill Posener, eds. (Freedom Editions)

One of the better photography books I came across celebrating the female form and lesbian sex. The book is loaded with beautiful images of women ranging from subdued to artsy to sexy to shocking.

Odd Girl Out–Ann Bannon (Cleis Press)

A shy and polite college girl has a stormy affair with her more outgoing and outrageous room mate. This book is a sleazy and twisted foray into the lesbian world of sex, done in the flawless pulp fiction style Bannon is famous for.

On Our Backs: The Best Erotic Fiction–Lindsay McClune, ed. (Alyson Books)

This book compiles the best erotic stories that have appeared in *On Our Backs* (a lesbian sex magazine) over its proud 20-year history. The writing is educational and hot and leaves no stone unturned.

Orgasm XL–Tony Ward (Last Gasp)

A book full of gritty and gorgeous photographs depicting lots of sexy women doing all sorts of raunchy things to each other. In color and black and white.

Rubyfruit Jungle–Rita Mae Brown (Bantam Books)

This classic coming-of-age story chronicles the life of a young girl from a poor southern family in the late 1950s. The story is about her bold coming-out as a lesbian, her many lovers, and her quest to find her place in the world. It's a short, easy read that's as funny as it is moving.

Sex Toy Tales–Anne Semans and Cathy Winks, eds. (Down There Press)

A fabulous book of stories about sexual adventures with things like vibrators, blenders, fishing lures, and computer joysticks. Stories range from okay to great and feature straight, gay, solo, and group sex.

Some Girls–Kristin McCloy (Plume)

A shy, straight country girl from New Mexico moves to New York City and has a hot and complicated relationship with her mysterious, cosmopolitan straight-girl neighbor. The story is well-written, erotic, and gripping and it deals with a lot of issues women have wrapping their heads around being with other women.

Tipping the Velvet–Sarah Waters (Riverhead Books)

A great novel about lesbian self-discovery in Victorian England. Waters is an awesome writer and this is a great read that you'll fly through–a fully compelling story with steamy sex scenes and great period detail.

Written on the Body–Jeanette Winterson (Vintage)

A love story between the narrator, whose gender and name are never revealed, and a married woman. A stunningly erotic and philosophical read.

Books to Show You How

First-Person Sexual: Women and Men Write About Self-Pleasuring–Joani Blank, ed. (Down There Press)

Fascinating and honest essays on masturbation by a bunch of really talented male and female writers.

Good Vibrations: The New Complete Guide to Vibrators—Joani Blank with Anne Whidden (Down There Press)

A tiny but thorough guide to all that vibrates from the founder of the hallowed sex shop. It covers the history of the vibrator, oldies but goodies, how to shop on a budget, questions and concerns, and much more.

Lesbian Sex Secrets for Men—Jamie Goddard and Kurt Brungardt (Plume)

Co-written by a queer woman and a straight man, this book is an interesting and thorough study on how women work and what they want. Even though it's written for men, pretty much everything in it is useful to anyone getting it on with a woman. It features information culled from focus groups as well as the authors' own experiences, and gives many a valuable blow-by-blow description on what to do in the sack.

The Lesbian Sex Book—Wendy Caster; revised by Rachel Kramer Bussel (Alyson Books)

A thorough and educated look at such important topics as women's health, relationships, gender politics, strap-on sex, good sex positions, and much more. It's easy to read, to the point, and contains artsy photographs and helpful illustrations.

The On Our Backs Guide to Lesbian Sex—Diana Cage, ed. (Alyson Books)

This book is a collection of some of the best works published over the years in the renowned lesbian magazine *On Our Backs*. It includes pieces on oral sex, BDSM, kissing, and strap-on sex, as well as some really hot photos.

Sex Toys 101—Rachel Venning and Claire Cavanah (Fireside)

A sassy, funny, and well-educated foray through the world of sex toys from the founders of the sex store Toys in Babeland. Full of great pictures and helpful tips.

SM 101—Jay Wiseman (Greenery Press)

A great place to start for those interested in taking a walk on the wild side. Wiseman has taught SM for 25 years and expertly walks you through how to find a partner, how to negotiate what you want, and how to get it on. He also provides helpful checklists that you can fill out for things such as limits, poses, and STDs.

Threesome: How to Fulfill Your Favorite Fantasy—Lori E. Gammon with Bill Strong (Triad Press)

This excellent, easy-to-read book covers all you need to know about getting it on with two people at once. It delves into the pros and cons of three-ways, discusses how to wrap your head around them and how to arrange them with friends, lovers, and strangers, the different kinds of people who are into them, and much more.

Tickle Your Fancy: A Woman's Guide to Sexual Self-Pleasure–Sadie Allison (Tickle Kitty Press)

I love this little book. It has great drawings, it's easy to read, and it's full of good ideas on how to get yourself off. It gives you information on techniques, toys, setting the mood, shaving your pussy, and much more.

Toygasms–Sadie Allison (Tickle Kitty Press)

A tiny but mighty sex toy guide with excellent drawings and info on things like getting ready for sex toy play, lubes, and much more. It's well-written and easy to read.

Tricks to Please a Woman–Jay Wiseman (Greenery Press)

For about a decade Jay Wiseman, a best-selling author and sex educator, has been writing a series of books on how to make sex better. This book contains the best tips he's collected over the years and presents them in quick little snippets. It's not the most thorough book, more like sex at a glance, but it gets to the point and delivers useful advice on fingering, oral sex, anal sex, toys, and much more.

The Ultimate Guide to Adult Videos–Violet Blue (Cleis Press)

An excellent guide to anything and everything smutty under the sun, this book provides insight on how to watch and select your videos and DVDs. It also has great reviews and a brilliant rating system that lets you know which films have unsightly boob jobs, real female orgasms, intense chemistry, and extreme sex acts, among other things.

The Ultimate Guide to Anal Sex for Women–Tristan Taormino (Cleis Press)

An avid fan of anal sex, Taormino covers everything from the physical to the psychological aspects of this fabulous pastime. She provides great information on trust, preparation, and toys, as well as dispelling myths about the act. The book also features testimonials from women who've tried it.

The Ultimate Guide to Cunnilingus–Violet Blue (Cleis Press)

This reader-friendly book provides great information on anatomy, safety, positions, technique, and more. It has helpful illustrations as well as quotes from avid pussy munchers. A terrific book to demystify this glorious sex act.

The Ultimate Guide to Strap-on Sex–Karlyn Lotney (Cleis Press)

A must-have for anyone interested in getting the most out of strapping it on. Written by a sex educator and former sex shop employee, it pretty much tells you everything you need to know about positions, equipment, lube, logistics, and more.

The Whole Lesbian Sex Book: A Passionate Guide for All of Us–Felice Newman (Cleis Press)

A thorough guide through women's sexuality and all it entails physically and psychologically. This book will answer many a burning question, like how to play with someone else's boobs, what to do with clits, strap-ons, and buttholes, and much, much more.

The Woman's Guide to Sex on the Web–Anne Semans and Cathy Winks (HarperCollins)

These women really did their homework and discovered a plethora of ways that the horny girl can benefit from the World Wide Web. The book takes you from how to use your computer to how to have cyber sex and lets you in on good sex education sites, chat rooms, online sex toy stores, the best date sites, and much more.

Bisexuality and the Eroticism of Everyday Life–Marjorie Garber (Routledge)

This book really stands out in a sea of dry, academic musings on the vast and complicated topic of sexuality. Marjorie Garber teaches at Harvard University and writes with incredible wit and knowledge about the cultural, scientific, literary, and psychological definitions of bisexuality. She did an excellent job of keeping my interest all the way through–which is saying something, because this book is huge and I'm kind of lazy.

The Clitoral Truth–Rebecca Chalker (Seven Stories)

This small and solid book takes an in-depth look at women's sexual anatomy and experiences. It reaches back to the early days of the clit, when she was first discovered, and her turbulent journey through the male-centered heterosexual model of sexuality. The book has excellent illustrations and plenty of information on how to excite, please, and understand the clit.

The Femme's Guide to the Universe–Shar Rednour (Alyson Books)

This book is really for femme lesbians, not straight

chicks, but we can all learn from each other and this is a great place to do it because Rednour's book is funny as hell, very playful, and full of useful pictures and information. She tells you how to work it as a girly girl in the lesbian scene, hands over some valuable sex tips (including what to do when your wrist gets tired), and much more.

Sex for One: The Joy of Selfloving–Betty Dodson, Ph.D. (Three Rivers Press)

The godmother of masturbation (this woman has dedicated her life to the subject) delves deep into the psychological, cultural, emotional, and physical aspects of masturbation. Although she does offer some tips, this book is more a cerebral look at self-pleasure, providing insight on liberating oneself, fantasy, shame, and much more. It also comes with impressive drawings done by Dodson herself.

Susie Sexpert's Lesbian Sex World–Susie Bright (Cleis Press)

A compilation of personal essays from the ever sassy and brilliant Susie Bright. The book's made up of Susie's wise observations from over the years on things such as politics, censorship, fisting, relationships, G-spots, and all sorts of other lesbianesque stuff. She offers a very insightful piece on the lesbian perils of sleeping with straight chicks, which should be required reading for all of us.

Get It Online

Sex Stores

www.adameve.com

A very thorough site selling everything from sex toys, novelties, books, videos, DVDs, video streaming, and more. It offers good reviews and links to other sex-related sites.

www.blowfish.com

This is definitely one of my favorite sites. It's got plenty of information, superb reviews of toys, books, and movies, and tons of sex toys and other sex-related paraphernalia for sale. It's brilliantly written and after going to site after site it was refreshing to find one with such a distinct and hilarious voice.

www.comeasyouare.com

A very groovy Canadian coop-run sex store with good books, toys, information and an excellent collection of silicone toys. Their stores are in Toronto and Montreal, but for those of us in different countries the website is pretty damn sufficient.

www.extracurious.com

Although this site sounds like it's geared toward the bi-curious, it's actually geared towards all women who are curious about learning about their bodies and their sexualities. It's a little on the dry side and smaller than most sites, but very pro-woman and pro-sex. It's got a decent selection of toys and books to buy, along with a bunch of interesting feminist-type knickknacks.

www.libida.com

An online shop by and for women. It's got invaluable information on things like nipple stimulation, cunnilingus, vibrators, and much more, as well as a wide selection of toys, books, and videos for sale. It provides sexperts to answer your questions and will even give you your horoscope, too!

www.mypleasure.com

A super site, with tons of quality toys and books for sale as well as good sex advice and health information. It's got an extensive Q & A section that deals with everything from lubrication issues to masturbation; reader polls; and interesting articles on things like positions and oral tricks.

www.newsensations.com

This site has a huge selection of videos and DVDs for sale as well as information and reviews. If you join the site, you can download a variety of hardcore pictures as well as stream dirty videos.

www.searchextreme.com

An excellent site that lets you shop for porn via performer, fetishes, production studio, director, setting, girl-on-girl, etc. It gives descriptions of each movie with a scene-by-scene breakdown of what goes on, including where the "money shot" is. One of the best sites I found for investigating and shopping for porn.

www.vixencreations.com

A woman-run online store specializing in premium silicone toys. It's definitely the place to go if you know you want to get something high quality. They also sell books, lubes, harnesses, vibrators, and more.

Note: Also see the Real Live Sex Stores section for the urls to some of the best sex shops.

Sex Information

www.clitical.com

A great site focusing on women's sexual pleasure. It includes tips on masturbation, dating, and sex toys. It also has a wide variety of chat rooms, reader submissions, product reviews, and more. A really excellent thorough site.

www.clublez.com

A site focused on the best lesbian love scenes in movies. You can join their discussion group and offer your opinions on movies or read up and get suggestions on what you want to rent or buy. It's a pretty limited site, but it can be helpful.

www.lezlovevideo.com

I can't recommend this site enough! It features a huge selection of girl-on-girl videos complete with synopses and reviews. This *so* helpful if you're overwhelmed by the infinite number of porn movies available, because the reviews are well-written and very detailed, and most have several opinions submitted by various readers. They sell lesbian-oriented sex toys, too.

www.mymasturbation.com

This site contains pages and pages of readers' masturbation stories with good info on toys, lubes, and other websites. It's a little heavy on the advertising level but still a very informative, good site that's fun to read.

www.scarletletters.com

A woman-run, sex-positive site that publishes erotic fiction, nonfiction, poetry, visual art, and more. The site also provides discussion forums and sex advice.

www.sexuality.about.com

A really impressive site that links you to just about any information you need in the sex realm. They sometimes have dopey articles on the home page, but don't let that turn you off—it's a very helpful site.

www.solotouch.com

A site full of the best-written reader masturbation stories I came across. Offers good articles and information and is a great place to go for ideas, turn-ons, and the feeling that you're not alone in your masturbational joy.

www.tinynibbles.com

Violet Blue, sex educator and revered author, packs her

site with book reviews, movie reviews, sex education, and advice on porn, rimming, cunnilingus, and much more. She also provides links to some of the more interesting sites on the web.

www.planetoutcom

This is a fabulous, huge site serving the lesbian, gay, bi, and transgender community. It provides information on entertainment, news, families, health, dating, travel, and much more.

Sex Services

www.adultfriendfinder.com

People who want sex partners looking for the same on-line. There is no small talk on this site. Pay a nominal fee, slap up a picture of your naked ass, describe how you want to get it, and you're on your way. Rates range from $4.90 a month to $29.95 a month, depending on how into the site you want to get.

www.cakenyc.com

A very feminist, pro-sex site that throws women-run erotic parties in New York. It has interesting articles that are available to the public for free and if you want to go deeper into what they have to offer you can pay $100 to join and gain entry to their parties (which include both men and women).

www.climaxcorner.com

For 10 bucks a month you can download as much porn as you want. Choose from amateur, anal, Asian, fetish, interracial, lesbian, teen, and oral. This is one of the least expensive porn downloading sites I've come across.

www.craigslist.org

I love this site. It's basically an online bulletin board where you can find concert tickets, buy cars, and for our purposes, find dates, log on to the sex forums, and browse the community section for possible lady-type goings on. If you post a personal ad here, it's not like most online sites where you have to fill out a profile—this is more freeform and you just write whatever you want. And it's free!

www.lavalife.com

When you join Lavalife's dating service, you have to fill out a profile for either dating, relationships, or intimate encounters, depending on what you're looking for. Then you search the site for those who've signed up for the same and contact them, which costs you credits, which cost you money depending on how many you want.

www.match.com

An online dating site that requires you to fill out a super-detailed, incredibly time-consuming profile. You can just post your profile and picture up there and wait for someone to contact you, but if you browse around and find someone you want to write, you must join for one month, three months, or six months. The monthly fees are prorated–the longer you join for, the cheaper the per-month fee.

www.nerve.com

This dating site requires you to fill out a very simple profile and is free to those who just want to post their stats. In order to contact someone, you have to buy a credit, which are sold in packs of 25, 50, or 100 from $24.95 to $69.95.

Real Live Great Stores

These are all sex-positive, mostly woman-run sex stores around the country that sell top-quality toys, accessories, books, safe-sex paraphernalia, and much more. Many provide sex workshops and have helpful, educated sales staffs to answer your questions. Notice that most of them have websites, too.

Come Again Erotic Emporium
    353 E. 53rd St.
    New York, NY 10022
    212-308-9394

Eve's Garden
    www.evesgarden.com
    119 W. 57th St. #420
    New York, NY 10019
    212-757-8651
    800-848-3837

Fetishes Boutique
    www.fetishesboutique.com
    704 S. 5th St.
    Philadelphia, PA 19147
    215-829-4986

Forbidden Fruit
    www.forbiddenfruit.com
    108 East North Loop Blvd.
    Austin, TX 78751
    800-315-2029

Good Vibrations

www.goodvibes.com

603 Valencia St. (at 17th St.)

San Francisco, CA 94110

(415) 522-5460

also:

1620 Polk St. (at Sacramento St.)

San Francisco, CA 94109

(415) 345-0400

also:

2504 San Pablo Ave. (at Dwight Way)

Berkeley, CA 94702

(510) 841-8987

Grand Opening!

www.grandopening.com

8442 Santa Monica Blvd.

West Hollywood, CA

323-848-6970

toll-free 877-731-2626

also:

318 Harvard St. Suite 32

Brookline MA 02446

617-731-2626

Intimacies
   www.intimacies.com
   28 Center St.
   Northampton, MA 01060
   413-582-0709

It's My Pleasure
   3106 NE 64th
   Portland, OR 97213
   503-280-8080

The Pleasure Chest
   7733 Santa Monica Blvd.
   West Hollywood, CA
   323-650-1022

Toys in Babeland:
   www.babeland.com
   707 E. Pike St.
   Seattle, Washington 98122
   206-328-2914
   also:
   94 Rivington St.
   New York, NY 10002
   212-375-1701

A Woman's Touch

www.a-womans-touch.com

600 Williamson St.

Madison, WI

53703

Movies With Good Lesbian Scenes/Themes

Aimée & Jaguar

A German housewife and a Jewish lesbian fall deeply and dangerously in love during World War II. Based on a true story, this movie is beautiful and sexy and will make you sob like a baby. In German with subtitles.

Better Than Chocolate

A young artist and her brand-new girlfriend take on censorship, hate crimes, and uninvited family members who come to live with them. This is a very sexy and fun movie that's got some super-hot moments between the two lead characters.

Bound

A gangster's girlfriend (Jennifer Tilly) falls for the butch ex-con (Gina Gershon) who's staying in the apartment next door. This movie is loaded with sexual tension, hot sex scenes, and suspense, and even though I found a lot of the Mafia stuff kind of hokey I really liked it. I highly recommend it for straight chicks since it does a great job of depicting how sex really goes down between two women, both of whom are gorgeous.

But I'm a Cheerleader

A highly hilarious and cartoony movie about a young cheerleader showing signs of gayness who gets sent away to some crazy camp where she's supposed to get deho-moized.

Chasing Amy

This hilarious movie might be more aptly titled *The Straight Dude's Guide to Sleeping with Lesbians*. Ben Affleck stars as a guy who falls in love with a lesbian who just happens to have the most irritating voice in film history. Once you get over her voice, though, you can appreciate that the movie's really well written, with lots of interesting musings about sexuality.

Claire of the Moon

A film about a group of handsome women at a writers' retreat who pretty much spend every waking hour discussing sexuality. It has some good sexual tension (and, eventually, hot sex scenes) between the two main characters, Ms. Straightypants and her handsome roommate, that luckily happen late enough in the movie so you have time to get used to the unbelievably terrible acting.

Desert Hearts

Once you recover from the scary title, you'll be amazed at what a good movie this is. An older, uptight, attractive straight woman gets together with a younger, free-spirited, foxy lesbian. Well written and well acted and very fun to watch, even though it kind of craps out at the ending. It does a great job of portraying some of the issues that arise when lesbians and straight women get together.

Foxfire

A group of misfit high school girls are inspired by a butch and mysterious outsider (Angelina Jolie) to join forces against the sexual abuses of a teacher. Based on the controversial novel by Joyce Carol Oates, this is a wonderful movie about female empowerment and friendship, with sexy, tension-filled moments between Angelina Jolie and several of the girls.

French Twist (Gazon maudit)

That Victoria Abril chick who's in a lot of Pedro

Almodovar's movies plays an unsatisfied, sexy housewife who gets it on with a butch truckdriver whose truck breaks down outside her house. Very sexy and funny.

Frida

Salma Hayek plays the famous bisexual artist Frida Kahlo. She's hot and sexy and there are some steamy scenes between her and the ladies. A beautiful movie to watch.

Gia

A true story about a fucked-up lesbian supermodel on a path to self-destruction, brilliantly portrayed by Angelina Jolie. It paints a painful and realistic picture of Gia's chaotic, drug-addled life, with plenty of steamy sex scenes between her and her straight girlfriend to balance it out.

Go Fish

An indie film sensation from 1994 about a group of lesbians living in Chicago, made by a group of lesbians living in Chicago. It's kind of dated and corny now but still sweet and romantic, and both actresses in it are sexy.

Heavenly Creatures

An awesome movie, based on a true story and starring

Kate Winslet. The film follows two semi-insane high school girls and their sexually charged, fantasy-fueled relationship. There are great erotic scenes and even a murder.

Henry and June

This is an amazing movie about Henry Miller, his wife, June (Uma Thurman), and the bisexual erotica writer Anaïs Nin (Maria de Medeiros), who comes between them. Well written, beautifully shot, and super-erotic, with great girl-on-girl tension between Thurman and de Medeiros.

High Art

Ally Sheedy plays a recovering addict lesbian photographer who gets it on with her infatuated, dippy, straight-girl neighbor. Very drug-scenestery and slow, but likable, especially for Patricia Clarkson's turn as a washed-up, drag-queeny German actress.

The Incredible True Story of Two Girls in Love

A cute, well-done movie about two teenage girls falling in love. One is more cultured and nervous and the other is trashy and uninhibited. Fun to watch, with lots of endearing, first-time awkwardness.

Kissing Jessica Stein

I recognize this movie's importance as one of the only mainstream straight-girl-goes-lesbian films, but I wish it was more believable! Although there are many great things about it, there is zero sexual tension between the straight lead character and her hot-as-hell first-ever girlfriend. It does cover some solid ground on lesbian bed death and sexual self-discovery and deals well with the awkwardness of coming out.

Like Water for Chocolate

A surreal, Gabriel-Garcia-Marquez-esque movie chronicling the lives of a family living in rural Mexico. One of the characters is a lesbian who gets together with her daughter's teacher in a very steamy scene.

Personal Best

A classic 1982 film about a pair of women athletes who meet at the 1976 Olympic trials and have an affair. It stars Mariel Hemingway as the innocent newcomer and a real-live U.S. Olympic Team veteran, Patrice Donnelly, as her older, more experienced lover.

Show Me Love (Fucking Åmål)

A totally adorable movie about a tortured loner high

school girl and her big fat crush on one of the most popular girls in school. Lesbian or not, anybody who lived through high school can relate. It's in Swedish, so you have to deal with subtitles, but it's well worth it.

Queen Christina

This 1933 classic stars Greta Garbo as the notoriously butch, cross-dressing Queen Christina of Sweden. For its time, this movie was quite shocking, what with all its gender ambiguity and sexual tension.

When Night Is Falling

A mythology professor at a conservative religious college takes off on an erotic adventure with an eccentric and gorgeous circus performer, putting her job and her relationship with her minister boyfriend on the line. Both the women in this film are gorgeous, the chemistry is hot, and the story is interesting. I really liked this one.

Porn

Directors

Andrew Blake (Studio A Entertainment/www.andrew-blake.com)

Blake's movies are where high art meets porn. Instead of the all-out fuckfests created by most directors, Blake focuses on fetish, tension, ambiance, and beauty. He uses gorgeous lighting, stunning women, and a keen eye to create the artsiest-fartsiest porn around. A lot of the scenes in his movies are women just playing with themselves, but they do get it on with each other and they're all really beautiful, so they're worth checking out. He's got a slew of titles out, but some to look for are:

Blondes and Brunettes: Sexy centerfolds revel in the world of high-class fetishism.

Delirious: A French heiress seduces her cousin and turns her boyfriend into a sex slave.

Dollhouse: A living, breathing sex doll indulges in all her food, smoking, and fetish fantasies.

Girlfriends: A group of gorgeous, statuesque women engage in all sorts of fetish play.

Hard Edge: A highly erotic, all-girl foray into a world where reality and fantasy collide.

Justine: A group of supermodels take an erotic tour of New York City's smutty underground.

Les Femmes Erotiques: Three hot women live out their sexual fantasies using toys, high-tech virtual-reality equipment, and each other.

Paris Chic: A gorgeous young filmmaker gets it on

with a hot young model who eventually becomes her sex slave.

Veronica Hart (VCA)

A porn star turned director, Veronica Hart is known for her story-driven movies and high production values. She gets some of the better actors in the business and creates sexual tension between the characters, rather than just having them jump right in and go at it. Her stuff is mostly straight-oriented, but has plenty of girl-on-girl action to satisfy the curious.

Sinful Rella: This movie is a campy spoof of the popular fairy tale. It's packed with great period costumes and hilarious scenarios, like when Rella blows Prince Charming and parties down at the ball with a bunch of horny lords and ladies.

Taken: An unhappy, wealthy housewife is abducted and taken to the mansion of a horny stranger; she fucks him and a bunch of other men and women. Full of suspense, twists, and seductions.

White Lightning: A sexy parole officer spends an action-packed 24 hours dealing with sordid criminals, blackmail, and temptation.

Michael Ninn (Pure Play Media/www.ninnworx.com)

Ninn fancies himself an artist more than a porn director, and it shows in his beautifully lit, moody films. He has an extensive catalogue. Some to watch out for:

Fem Bella: A highly erotic, fetish-based movie about a bunch of hot femme chicks seducing each other.

Diva Girls: A glossy movie of mostly hot women doing naughty things to themselves in different outfits. There's also some hot girl-on-girl, but mostly solo play. Great for those learning to masturbate or wanting fantasy material about other chicks masturbating.

Diva Volume 4: The last in a four-part series, this movie has plenty of solo action, girl-on-girl, and role-playing. Great costumes and sets shot with classic Ninn glossiness.

Shar Rednour and Jackie Strano
(Sir Video/www.sirvideo.com)

Girlfriends Rednour and Strano write, direct, and act in their movies, all of which are 100 percent dyke produced. I like these movies because they have a sense of humor and feature women who not only enjoy fucking women, but who know how to do it well. Don't expect the usual cast of boob-jobbed, fingernailed straight-girl porn stars you're used to, because these movies were made by and for dykes.

Hard Love: This movie is about a pair of ex-girlfriends

who can't resist fucking each other. It's a fabulous foray into lesbian sex complete with femmes, butches, and excellent strap-on scenes. It features many hot women and decent acting.

How to Fuck in High Heels: This movie was based on a live performance piece of Shar's and shows you how to fuck in style. It provides an erotic education on strap-ons, group sex, shoe worship, and much more.

Sugar High Glitter City: A futuristic story about sugar becoming outlawed and the sugar-addicted dykes who'll do anything to get their hands on some.

Series

The 4 Finger Club
(New Sensations/ www.newsensations.com)

This series shows hot girls getting it on in unscripted performances. It has them in groups and one-on-one, using toys, tongues, and lots of fingers. The series has 21 films in all and in a lot of them the girls get off for real, which is a rare bonus.

No Man's Land
(Video Team/www.videoteam.com)

With a whopping 38 movies, this all-girl series dates

back to 1988. The stories are all based around lesbian or bisexual characters, and even though some of them are the boob-jobbed, fingernailed ones we're so used to seeing in straight films, at least they're targeting homo and bi audiences! This series also has Asian editions, Latin editions, and European editions.

Shane's World
(Digital Sin/www.shanesworld.com)

Reality TV meets porn in this 34-part film series conceived and directed by porn star extraordinaire Shane. The films depict groups of horny people taking over various locations and fucking each other's brains out. Titles include *Rollercoaster of Love*, *Keg Party*, *Campus Invasion*, and *Scavenger Hunt* (where they run around LA and fuck in different places). It's your standard porn with lots of girl-on-girl, boy-on-girl, and group, but I recommend it for its unrehearsed, hilarious run-around style.

Slumber Party
(Digital Sin/www.shanesworld.com)

This extensive series chronicles Shane (who directs as well) and her rowdy girlfriends getting it on, and on, and on. It's 19 films of girl porn for as far as the eye can see that's pretty consistently hot and rarely wastes time on things like plot and characters. The women are usually fairly normal-looking with the occasional stripper type tossed in.

Where the Boys Aren't (Vivid)

This rowdy series of 16 films dates back to 1989. The movies are all girl-on-girl and generally have decent lighting and production values; they feature some of the biggest names in porn. These movies are pretty much just scene after scene of Playmate-type babes fucking, and most of them are pretty hot.

Women Seeking Women
(Girlfriends Films/www.girlfriendsfilms.com)

This tiny but mighty series (so far there are eight movies in the collection) contain different vignettes of different girls getting it on. These movies stand out because the girls are normal, not porn-star types, and many of them obviously enjoy fucking each other. All the movies pay attention to things like mood, lighting, and foreplay and the majority of women in them are real-life lovers or at least friends.

Movies

Bad Wives (Paul Thomas/Vivid)

A couple of bored housewives spice things up by tag-teaming the buff supermarket check-out boy. Lots of three-way action, girl-on-girl, and anal sex.

Beat the Devil (Robb D./Digital Playground)

A movie about a guy who sells his soul to the devil. Complete with standard semi-scary porno acting, plot twists, girl-on-girl sex, flames, and techno music.

Jenna Loves Kobe (Vivid/www.clubsienna.com)

Two popular femme porn stars get it on with each other and a bunch of other men and women. Pretty typical porn, but I thought the chicks were hot, and some of the girl-on-girl sex was particularly steamy.

The Lesbian Couple Volume 1
(Erockta Vision/erocktavision.com)

This movie focuses just as much on the fucking as it does on finding super-hot lesbians, great lighting effects, and rockin' music.

Real Girlfriends #1
(RealGirl Video/www.realgirlvideos.com)

Two young girls who are actually girlfriends and are actually hot for each other shot this amateur video of themselves having sex. It's pretty damn good as far as amateur porn goes because the production value is decent, the sex is steamy, and they look like they're enjoying themselves.

Red Vibe Diaries–Object of Desire
(directed by James Avalon/Cal Vista Films)

A rich Beverly Hills housewife fulfills her fantasy of becoming a prostitute at a brothel. The film has lots of great costumes, plenty of girl-on-girl and boy-girl sex, and acting that, by porn standards, isn't too painful.

Seven Deadly Sins
(Vivid/www.vividvideo.com)

A sex party in hell, full of lustful vixens, toys, threeways, and plenty of girl-on-girl.

acknowledgments

It's hard to pick an order to thank people in because everyone who helped with this book helped so much I'd hate for it to sound like I was placing anyone's importance above anyone else's. So I'm going to thank them all in height order (tallest to shortest). These are the sweet and amazing people I'm hugely grateful to for helping me out:

Rembert Block who did all the awesome illustrations in exchange for a knitted shrug. I'm only sorry I didn't need an opera diva accordionist for my book as well because then I could have utilized her talents more fully.

The ever-supportive Peter Steinberg whose enthusiasm about this project from day one kept me going. He was always there when I needed him with advice, humor, and calming words when my neurosis took over. He also took me out for dinner every time he was in town.

Amanda Patten for her insight, humor, and super-human ability to take this once-sloppy mess and turn it into a readable piece of smut. I do not know how she does it but she does it really well.

Stacy Jill and Kim Airs at the fabulous Los Angeles sex boutique, Grand Opening, who let me sit in their store for hours and do research. They also answered my eight million questions and opened early one day so I could photograph their sex toys.

Angela Ellsworth for feeding me cheese and taking my picture in the bathtub of her fancy Pasadena home.

Jolanta Benal and everyone else at Simon & Schuster whose hard work made this book possible.

All the friends and family members who suffered through my inappropriate questions about their sex lives. I am blown away by their honesty. And their studliness.

And last but not least, the anonymous swarm of incredible women and men who let me interview them. It was beyond inspiring that these strangers not only took the time to help me out, but that they divulged such intimate and graphic details of their lives with such articulate shamelessness. Not only did they provide me with valuable information to use in my book and my life, but they gave me hope that there are people out there who can talk about sex as the vital, natural, fun thing it is. Thank you thank you thank you!